ACHIEVING SUCCESS IN AMERICA

ACHIEVING SUCCESS IN AMERICA

IF AN 18 YEAR OLD PENNILESS IMMIGRANT COULD DREAM BIG, YOU CAN TOO.

SID BARON

EXXEL PUBLISHING

Achieving Success in America
If an 18 Year Old Immigrant Could Dream Big, You Can Too!

Published by:
Exxel Publishing Co.
323 Telegraph Rd.
Bellingham, WA 98226
Tel.: 360-671-2275
Toll free: 1-877-939-1999

Quotes from conversations included within the text represent the recollections of the author and are within the scope of what was discussed even though they may not be exactly as spoken, word-for-word.

Ordering information:
Visit www.exxelpublishing.com for easy on-line ordering.
Contact author via E-mail: sietze@msn.com
Mail your order to:
Exxel Publishing Co.
323 Telegraph Rd.
Bellingham, WA 98226

Inquire about quantity discounts.
Ordering by telephone or fax:
Telephone: 360-671-2275
Toll free: 1-877-939-1999
Fax: 360-671-7616

ISBN 978-0-9897391-0-8

Printed in the U.S.A.

2020 2019 2018 2017 2016 2015 2014

DEDICATION

At this stage of my life I've already lived beyond the current life expectancy for men in the U.S. Had I been unhappy and not enjoyed the journey of my life with my dear wife and best friend Margaret I might never have started writing. Margaret always understood the many times I didn't hear when she was talking to me because I was thinking about writing.

For more than 60 years Margaret has been a part of the journey and fabric of my life.

As her husband, the father of our six children, the provider, she has always energized me to be the best I could be in every area of my responsibilities. We share a passion for helping others. We rejoice when our generosity and the blessings of our lives touch the lives of our loved ones, family members, friends and even strangers. We are now in the sunset of our lives and when the golden cords that bond us to our mortal lives will break, it will not be our achievements, wealth or accomplishments that will matter. It will be the care and clarity with which we have loved each other that will speak of God's amazing grace in giving us the gift of each others lives. Thank you Margaret.

Sid Baron

TABLE OF CONTENTS

INTRODUCTION

In America, Hard Times Lead to New Prosperity

When the so-called Great Recession started in late 2007, the lives of most Americans were affected. As someone in his early 80s who has seen the effects of the Great Depression, lived in wartime Holland during World War II and immigrated to the United States in the late 1940s with nothing but the bare necessities, I have been blessed to have built several successful businesses while raising a large family.

The reason I wrote this book is to help those who are willing to work hard so that they, too, can live the American dream. Within this book are the principles I have dedicated myself to living. It is my hope that they will help you, the reader, to likewise enjoy a life filled with success and meaning.

Often when I meet young people they will tell me stories of struggling to make ends meet while living through our current difficult times. The story of one young man stands out. Over coffee he remarked: "Mr. Baron, you are a wealthy man who has enjoyed great success in your business and personal life. But no matter how hard I try, I can't seem to get ahead. Do you have any suggestions that can help me achieve success?"

I thought long and hard about what that young man was asking. My heart went out to him because he had seemingly lost all hope. At the same time I also knew if he followed the path I'd taken he, too, would find success. Even though our current times may seem difficult, the world has lived through worse.

When I was born in 1930, the world was in the midst of a depression never before seen. In the United States, unemployment peaked at over 25 percent while in the Netherlands, where I spent my first eighteen years, a similar percentage of people were without jobs.

Then in 1940, just as Holland was beginning to recover, my homeland was attacked by the Nazi's during the Battle of the Netherlands and remained occupied until 1945. After the wartime years, Holland found itself living with the ruins of war and faced with massive housing shortages, lack of food and no prospects for work. It was during those years, after the war, that my family decided to immigrate to the United States.

Though the United States was not attacked on its mainland during World War II, in large part it funded the war and sacrificed many of its sons and daughters. By the end of the war the national debt rose to 120 percent of its gross domestic product (GDP), which is even a higher percentage than the roughly 100 percent it is at today.

When our family arrived in the United States the rate of inflation was over 10 percent, triple the percentage of inflation today.

Putting Things into Perspective

Since the founding of the United States with the Declaration of Independence in 1776, there have been forty-six confirmed recessions. That equates to one recession every five years. In my lifetime I have lived through fourteen of them. My first was as a child in the Netherlands during the Great Depression of the 1930s and throughout World War II, and later during adulthood after my family immigrated to America. Though the recent so-called Great Recession of 2007-2009 was certainly horrible for those caught up in the subprime mortgage crisis and subsequent unemployment, there have been other recessions that were also devastating. Two of the worst were the recessions of 1973-1975 when oil prices quadrupled and unemployment shot up to 9 percent and the recession of 1981-1982 starting with the Iranian Revolution and resulting in stagflation—high interest rates coupled with a stagnant economy, inflation and high unemployment. The point is that recessions are a natural occurrence and that we need to be prepared.

Though recessions happen, the good news is that they are always followed by a time of economic expansion. Therefore, navigating the seesaw nature of worldwide economics requires individuals to always keep their personal finances in balance.

Fortune magazine, in a recent Fortune 500 edition, determined that 40 percent of listed companies were either founded by an immigrant or the children of an immigrant. The revenue generated by Fortune 500 companies founded by immigrants or children of immigrants is larger than the GDP of every other country in the world except China and Japan.

This is proof positive that those who immigrate to the United States are still able to live out the American dream.

If you are either new to our country or find yourself in a situation where things are not heading your way, it is important to know that in life we are often tested with less than ideal situations. However, in many other countries one's lot in life is determined very early on by family wealth (or lack thereof) or a person's place in society. Here in this country what was true decades ago is still true today. If you work hard, understand the business you are in or job you have and display a positive attitude, you have just as much of a chance to be successful as any other person in our country.

Recently, *The New York Times* ran a series of articles featuring debates about whether America was still the land of opportunity. Each debate focused on specific issues such as personal debt, education, wealth, inheritance and hard work. While there are many challenges in each of those areas, when it comes to entrepreneurialism, America is the best country in the world for taking an idea and turning it into a business.

My own story of immigrating to America after World War II with little more than a few belongings is one that is still possible today. Though today's immigrants are more likely to come from areas outside western Europe, the journey is very much the same.

Farewell to the Land of My Birth

My mother had two cousins who, along with their families, immigrated to the U.S. before the outbreak of World War II. After the war ended, and because of the devastation in the Netherlands and the rest of Europe, Mom's cousins were anxious to find out if she and her family survived. Soon letters started arriving and before long my parents were discussing moving to America. At the time I didn't pay much attention, nor was I the least bit interested in making such a life-changing move. Instead, as a young man who was nearly eighteen years old, I was more concerned about helping my dad make a success of our family farm. My lack of interest was also due to my other activities at the time including my electronics and honeybee businesses (not to mention the thought of leaving my girlfriend behind). I can remember Mom saying, "We think that emigrating might be best for our children's futures. But if you and your brother Henk aren't interested, we might drop the idea." From her remarks, it was apparent that she and Dad would be disappointed if we didn't go with them.

One day a bold headline in our weekly newspaper grabbed my attention. "Amerika. Land van Onbegrensde Mogelijkheden" (America, Land of Unlimited Opportunities). The article excited me. After work that evening I walked the short distance to our neighbors little bar and café. The owner, Mr. Boonstra, was easy to talk to and after I ordered a soft drink he sat down to chat. "I hear your parents are thinking of emigrating to America, Sietze. Is that true?"

"*Ja*, that's true, but I'm not at all excited about it, so it may not happen. That's just fine with me."

"What?" he said with incredulity. "You're not excited about it? You're crazy!" I asked him why. "You're a young man. It's an enormous adventure, and you can always come back and start your life here if you don't like it."

Prior to that I hadn't thought of it as an adventure, but after speaking with Mr. Boonstra it made a lot of sense. That night, when I returned home, I told Mom and Dad that I was in full agreement with their emigration plans. Soon I sold my bees, the inventory of honey and most of my electronics. Unfortunately the money didn't do me any good since I wouldn't be able to use it in America.

Early one morning, in late May 1948, our family, together with uncles and aunts and other close friends, filled a bus and headed to Rotterdam. That afternoon we boarded the S.S. Veendam, a Holland America cruise ship, and began our voyage to America. I still remember standing at the railing on the top deck and waving goodbye to my girlfriend who was walking along the shore waving the handkerchief she used to dry her tears, perhaps knowing we would never see each other again.

As the coastline of Holland disappeared in the distance I wondered if I'd ever see the land of my birth again. While pondering that question an announcement told us to gather in the dining room for dinner. It was the most beautiful dining room I had ever seen. As our family gathered around a table we were handed a menu which seemed to be in French, a language none of us could read. When the perfectly dressed waiter asked for my order I simply pointed at a menu item. Once my dinner arrived I had no idea what was on the plate. It certainly wasn't anything I'd eaten before. But it had been a long day and we were tired after being awake for many hours. After dinner we were shown our sleeping quarters which were nothing like the luxurious spacious guest rooms of present day cruise ships. Instead, ours was a tiny room equipped with two bunk beds. It didn't matter. We had nothing to compare it to, and that night my brother and I slept soundly.

The following morning after breakfast, my brother Henry and I decided to explore the ship. Standing at the railing of one of the upper decks all we saw was water. No coastlines anywhere, only ocean water with foaming waves as far as the eye could see. Later when our family gathered in the dining room for our first lunch at sea, mother was absent. Dad informed us she was not feeling well. As it turned out she would be seasick the entire eleven days of our trans-oceanic journey to our new home.

We soon discovered that many of the passengers aboard were also emigrating from Holland to America. It didn't take us too long to find some friends around our age from our homeland province of Friesland. I especially remember Hylke, who was a couple years older than me. He had relatives in the state of Wisconsin who were sponsoring him. I asked him what he did during the war years. Hylke told me that the last two years of the war he was in hiding with others who were active in the Dutch underground resistance movement. Even though he was a little too young to be directly involved in the movement, he knew they were hiding a man wanted by the Germans. If the Germans had found he was hiding the man his entire family would have been executed. He went on to explain that their group was involved in sabotaging German installations and recovering weapons dropped by the British Royal Air Force for use by the Freedom Fighters.

Hylke and I had a great talk and soon we were laughing like old friends. But after a while our laughter was drowned out by the sound of an ever-increasing wind howling up against the ship. I walked to the bow and leaned over the protective railing. The ship was pitching as it plunged into the waves only to rise again and repeat the pitching motion. It made me feel a little queasy. Now I understood why Mom was seasick. I decided to go to the cabin and lie down for a while. As I walked through the parlor I noticed several people enjoying tea and cookies. One elderly lady was sitting alone. She motioned for me to come over to her. "Can you get me a cup of tea?"

Though I didn't understand English the word tea is the same in both the Dutch and English languages. She pointed to where a waiter was pouring tea. I responded by bringing the lady a cup and placing it in front of her on the table. She smiled and reached over as though she wanted to shake hands. Instead what she wanted was to give me a tip for being kind and helpful to her. When I opened my hand after shaking hers, there, for the first time in my life, I saw an American dollar. I knew how to say "thank you" in English and did so, with a big smile. I felt rich.

When I woke up on Friday morning, June 4, 1948, I felt our ship slowing down and could no longer feel the rocking motion of the ocean. I said to my brother Henry, who was writing in his logbook, "We must be nearing our destination." He told me we were due to arrive in Hoboken, New Jersey. We decided to grab some breakfast at the buffet and then climb the stairs to the upper deck to have a look. As we walked past Mom and Dad's cabin we noticed they were both busy packing our suitcases. Henry and I raced up the stairways to the top deck. "Look Sid," Henry said with excitement in his voice, "There is the Statue of Liberty." We were awestruck. The famous symbol of freedom and liberty seemed so close and so huge. We were in America, the land of unlimited opportunities.

Early that afternoon we set foot in our adopted homeland for the first time. But our excitement was subdued because of the fear of the unknown. We headed to our first stop, which was at the Seaman's House—a mission that supplied food and other supplies to newly arrived immigrants. At the Seaman's House we were supplied sacks of sandwiches, which would be our only food during our long train ride west. Though at that time we did not realize it, the four-day train ride would literally bring us from the Atlantic Ocean to the Pacific Ocean. During our long train ride we sat, ate sandwiches and slept on our wooden train seats. We did not have money to enjoy any of the creature comforts available. At around seven in the morning, on June 8, 1948, we arrived in Seattle. Then, after boarding a different train, early that same afternoon we arrived in Bellingham, Washington where our family was greeted by one of my mother's cousins and her husband. From there they took us to their farm home in Everson. For the first time in over two weeks we enjoyed a delicious meal together as a family which had been wonderfully prepared by Mom's cousin, Jeanette Lankhaar.

Within a couple days my father and I got jobs on a large farm. Our family moved into a small unpainted house, which was more like a shack than a home. Life for us in America had just begun. There were several employees of the farm, none of whom was able to speak or understand Dutch. The foreman gave me the instructions for our work assignment and, after I understood what we needed to do, I explained it to my Dad in Dutch. I had no choice but to learn English quickly. Later I often regarded it as a blessing because I realized without learning to speak, read and write in the language of my new country, as flawlessly as possible, it would be impossible to realize the American dream of unlimited opportunities.

CHAPTER ONE

TAKE CHARGE OF YOUR LIFE:

ASSUMING RESPONSIBILITY FOR THE DECISIONS WE MAKE

I first met Sid through my work in maintenance at Meadow Greens Retirement Community in Lynden, Washington. From the beginning I could tell he was a successful man. Our first connection point was that both his daughter, Julie, and I were negatively impacted by drunk drivers. Sid helped me to prepare a monthly message to those recently charged with impaired driving.

Sid has been a father figure to me and helped our family through tough times. We regularly go out for lunch where he offers me advice and wisdom. Words can't express how special he is. I'm someone who grew up without a father and never received any guidance on taking charge of my finances. As a result, I accumulated a lot of credit card debt along with high interest car payments. Sid helped me understand how to correct my financial mistakes and, as a result, take charge of my life. He counseled me on how he would have handled my finances and helped me mange my money. Over the past few years I have not borrowed any money and my past debt is almost paid off. Like many people, my wife and I lived on our credit cards. In fact, at one time we had seven or eight different cards. As a result we struggled and were always short on cash.

Sid took me under his wing and showed me how to manage our budget. He also helped restructure our debt through low interest consolidation which allowed us to get rid of our credit cards. His plan turned everything around for us. We were no longer broke and out of money. Sid also helped us set up a monthly budget and to regularly put money into a savings account.

Did we follow his advice to the letter? Not always. Once I decided to take out a second car loan without telling him. One day over lunch I admitted my mistake. Rather than get angry he gave me a second chance. He even told a joke to relieve the tension. Through Sid's help I've learned to take charge of my life. As I said, he's been like a father to me. Beyond helping with my finances he has also been invaluable in my family and work life. Sid believes that each person should take charge of all aspects of their lives from choosing a vocation, having healthy relationships and managing finances.

—Zack DeBerry is team member of the Meadow Greens Retirement Community staff in Lynden, Washington. He serves primarily as maintenance director but has the skills to "pinch-hit" in every department.

Picking a Direction

When do career choices begin? Were there childhood clues as to what you'd become? What did you dream about when you were a kid? What were your interests? What games did you play? How did you spend your free time in the winter? What about summers? Did you read books, play games, or make sand castles?

When you were a kid how did you answer the question, "What do you want to be when you grow up?"

Often it's the things that we loved as a child that give us clues to our passions. For example, my brother loved playing schoolteacher. He pretended to grade imaginary students' work when he was growing up. What was his working lifetime career? After earning his teaching certificate he taught in a small Christian school in the state of Washington. At the same time he continued his education. His next step took him to Grand Rapids, Michigan where he accepted a position as high school teacher. Since he had a wife and small children he didn't have the luxury of continuing his education full-time. His determination to achieve the highest level in his chosen career eventually resulted in him earning a doctorate degree in English literature and becoming a professor at Calvin College in Grand Rapids. Teaching students was the culmination of his childhood dreams. Never ignore your childhood interests nor the fear of making career changes no matter how old you are now.

Many experts tell us that human beings do not generally have the ability to retain memories before the age of three. However some studies reveal that this is only partially correct. Even though we do not retain memories of those earliest years, infants learn more during the first three years of of life than any subsequent three-year period thereafter. This is because what is learned during that time period is retained on a subconscious level. A question to explore is: When are the first indications of the future career orientation of a child initially discernible?

Another question is, do school grades predict future career success? I didn't achieve good grades in many of my classes. I only received high grades when I concentrated on studying subjects I was interested in. In those subjects, even with minimum effort, I always received passing grades. When, in 2005, I was in Holland for the introduction of my book *The Way it Was*, which had been translated in the Dutch language, I was signing books during a promotion at Douma's bookstore in Surhuisterveen. I signed a book for a lady who looked about my age. Obviously she knew who I was because my Dutch name was on the front cover. She seemed to be studying my face and lingered until I had a brief break. "Do you remember me?" she asked. I studied her face but no spark of recognition ignited and I had to confess that I did not remember her. She said "Sietze (my Dutch name), you and I were in the first grade together. My name was Annie Zijlstra (not her real name). Don't you remember that our first grade teacher, Miss Schipper, always asked us to read the stories for the class?" I said, "No I don't remember that either. Why did we have to do that?" "Oh," she said with a sly grin which I interpreted as meaning she thought I was pretty dumb. Finally she answered my question. "Miss Schipper always asked us because we were the best readers in the class." All I remember about my time in school is that instead of concentrating on listening and learning, I spent many class hours dreaming about other things. However, I don't remember what I was curious about back then.

I was born on a small farm located in Opende, in the Netherlands, just on the border between the provinces of Groningen and Friesland. The year was 1930 and my early years were spent in the middle of a world-wide depression. Obviously I was unaware of the struggle for economic survival experienced by millions. However, I might have overheard snatches of conversations between my parents that subliminally conveyed to me that it wasn't easy for them to meet their obligations. Later my mom told me that my father had started a little feed and fertilizer business during the depression. That made it possible for him to barely make it by combining his income as both a small farmer and a small business owner. Mom explained that Dad was a very proud and responsible man who didn't want to take government hand-outs if he could possibly provide for his family himself. I have never forgotten that message of independence and responsibility. By telling me about my dad, my mother unwittingly unearthed within me a rough blueprint for my own life.

Reading must have come to me early and easily. I was probably still in first grade when I picked up a colorful little catalog with pictures of small packages of garden seeds. On the back page was an ad that grabbed my attention. "Earn money selling garden seeds to friends and neighbors." That became my first business venture. I could earn as much as a dime on some packages of seed but most only earned me a nickel. With a dime I could buy a hundred marbles. This was during a time when most school kids played with marbles but few had money to buy them. I sold twenty marbles for three cents and made a nickel every time I sold a hundred of them. Selling marbles felt good and allowed me to have a few nickels in my pocket.

Over the years people have often asked me: "When did you become an entrepreneur, Sid?" With a grin my answer has always been: "I was born an entrepreneur even before Webster put the word in his dictionary." Back when I sold marbles I was a little boy with no knowledge about business or entrepreneurship. However, I instinctively knew how to make a sale and earn a little money.

CHAPTER TWO

FOLLOW YOUR PASSION:

USING OUR UNIQUE GIFTS FOR A JOY-FILLED LIFE

When I was still in school, oftentimes I would drop by Baron Music and Electronics which was a new store at the time in Lynden, Washington. While there I'd spend hours looking through the classical music section to see which record to buy next. Years later, after college, I returned to Lynden to pursue a career in the radio broadcasting business. At the time, Sid owned a tiny FM station with offices next to Baron Music and Electronics. Remembering me from my earlier days hanging out in his store, Sid offered me a job working at the radio station. However, Sid also mentioned that he was negotiating to sell the station to someone else and that my job might not be permanent. In spite of his warning, I decided to take the job anyway. It was just good to have a job in radio, which was my passion. At that time, in the mid 1960s, FM radio was not yet popular and few stations made money. We decided something had to be done to attract more listeners as well as advertisers to the station. Sid and I worked well together because he is an idea man and I'm good with follow through and details.

One of Sid's ideas was to start broadcasting local sports, especially high school basketball. At the time nobody broadcast high school basketball games on the radio. I was responsible for hiring the play-by-play announcers, setting up the equipment and selling the ads. The idea turned out to be a hit and soon the radio station was making money. In fact it was so successful that in the next season we also added high school football.

I worked with Sid at the radio station for nearly twelve years and throughout that time he was my mentor. When I left to sell Allen Organs, and became the west coast distributor of church organs, Sid encouraged me and to this day we have remained good friends.

Sid gave me a chance to start my career, even though I lacked experience, which is something I'll always be thankful for. He also was my mentor and taught me how to sell. Sid stressed always calling on customers at the right time (when they needed what I sold), and to have something I believed in to sell.

—Jerry VanderPol, former FM station manager. He has sold his church organ business and is now retired. He remains in high demand as a church organist and choir director. He lives with his wife in the North Seattle area.

The Importance of Doing What We are Passionate About

Whether you are starting a business or deciding what career path to follow, it is important to follow your passions. In my life I have always done what both excited me and stirred my interests. While making money is important, it cannot be the sole determining factor when starting a business.

Putting Things into Perspective

When I was seven or eight, my dad showed me how to milk cows. As World War II raged on, milking the cows was something I did every morning no matter what was happening in our country. Of course, I would have preferred to continue my slumber for a couple of hours rather than get up at six o'clock to do it. Especially in the early spring when the weather was cold or rainy and the cows were no longer in the warm barn. I remember one morning in particular when Dad was either impatient, a little cranky, or both–probably because the cows were out in the field, some distance from the house.

That morning I dressed groggily in the dark room. The closed window drapes hid any view of the weather outside. Peeking through a slit in the drapes, I noticed it wasn't raining. It looked like it could be the beginning of a beautiful day in May just prior to me celebrating my tenth birthday.

While Dad was busy doing other chores, I loaded the wheelbarrow with two empty ten-gallon milk cans, two pails, and two milk stools. Dad opened the heavy wooden gate leading to the pasture where our small herd of black and white milk cows were peacefully grazing. Dew was heavy on the grass. Birds were chirping and searching for twigs or straws of dead grass to build their nests and raise a family of baby birds. Everywhere was evidence of new life beginning to show off the colors, smells, and beauty of an early spring day.

Dad, who was never talkative in the morning, pointed to one of the cows he wanted me to milk. I sat down on my milk stool with the bucket firmly lodged between my knees and began milking. That was when I first heard unfamiliar sounds coming from far away. Rarely was there any traffic this early in the morning. But now I could hear the sound of a truck engine coming down the road from the direction of Surhuisterveen. I stopped milking and looked toward the road, straining to see. Suddenly, there they were. Not just one truck, but five or six. They were not ordinary transport trucks but green, canvas-covered vehicles–military vehicles–and they were not paying attention to any speed limits.

Then I heard a distant explosion, followed by the deep, droning sound of many engines. I knew they must be airplanes, but I couldn't see them. They were not like the regular KLM passenger airplane that used to scare me while flying over our house each day. I looked in the direction where Dad was milking a cow. He looked back at me, but neither of us spoke. We both knew something highly unusual was happening. This peaceful spring morning had taken a scary twist. Dad quickly loaded the filled milk cans onto the wheelbarrow and we headed for the house. The remaining morning chores of feeding the pigs, chickens, and horse were delayed. I followed Dad inside where he promptly turned on the radio. He stood as if he was glued to the floor while waiting impatiently for the radio tubes to warm up. Finally we heard the announcer's voice, with its mixture of somber seriousness, excitement, and anxiety. Mom, who was setting the breakfast table, seemed to freeze into still frame as the news came over the airwaves. Hitler's armies and air force, the Luftwaffe, had crossed the borders of neutral Holland. Cities had been bombed. Many innocent people were dead and dying.

There had been talk that, sooner or later, Adolph Hitler might decide to turn his armies loose on the Netherlands. But the Netherlands had declared its neutrality and many Dutch believed Hitler would honor the declaration. On May 10, 1940, that trust was shattered when the Germans invaded. All my fears about Adolph Hitler and his deadly airplanes had now become real. I thought about Mr. Nobach, a local Nazi sympathizer, and the praise he had given Hitler while we were talking in the field. Would he still welcome Hitler into the Netherlands now that their forces had killed our countrymen? The carefree world of a ten-year-old had abruptly been replaced with a world where I would never again feel completely safe. After breakfast, as he did every morning, Dad reached for the Bible. It was such a regular custom that we kids rarely paid much attention. Usually, the serious expressions on our faces mostly reflected our pretension that we were listening. This morning was different. Dad read from Psalm 42: "Though an army shall rise up against me, I will fear no evil, for God is with us."

I listened to every word of that reading and of the prayer that followed. The dark clouds of war now hung over our country, over my life and the lives of my family. Would I survive? For how long? Would we get bombed? Would my little brother get killed, too? What about my sisters and parents? I was afraid. All the security and predictability of our daily existence was gone and replaced by an enormous fear of the unknown.

I walked outside and looked for a place of solitude. I sat down behind the barn, where no one could see me. Looking up into the sky, which had always been peaceful, I tried to see beyond the danger and hostility created by enemy aircraft. Far above the menace on planet earth was God. Kneeling, I talked to God, praying for the safety of my family and for an end to the war. But I had a frightening feeling that this day marked the beginning of much worse to come.

In 1943, when I was thirteen, my mother came home one day and placed her bicycle against the brick wall of the house and called me. "Sietze," she said, "Your grandpa's brother, my uncle Evert passed away." I could tell Mom was sad so I nodded sympathetically. I had met uncle Evert at least a couple times and could clearly envision the appearance of the round-faced, gray-haired elderly gentleman. Mom continued, "Sietze, when uncle Evert retired from his wooden shoe making business he became a beekeeper. There are about six boxes of hives full of honeybees. They don't know what to do with them. Are you interested in becoming a beekeeper and selling the honey after you harvest it?" As a young teenager I knew little about bees other than they can sting you. I remembered once walking across our small front lawn with bare feet and stepping on a clover flower not knowing that a bee was busy attempting to extract some nectar from the flower. That bee got me right on the bottom of my foot. It swelled up and hurt for three days. However, being able to harvest and sell honey sounded appealing. Maybe I would earn a little money. I studied long and hard to learn about the fascinating complex customs, work habits and social hierarchy of each family of bees living in a hive.

I had graduated from grade school at age thirteen and enrolled in a school of slightly higher learning. The school was some distance away and I had to board a small train daily to get to the small city of Drachten where it was located. By this time I had outgrown the age of "marbles." At the age of thirteen most boys started smoking. The war was still raging and real tobacco was not available. As a result, the kids rolled their own cigarettes using whatever could reasonably be substituted for tobacco. If someone had acquired some real tobacco on the "black market" many boys begged him to sell them just enough to roll a thin cigarette. I'd read a little about beekeepers using tobacco to calm their bees. Even though I'd only had the bees for a few days and had not yet opened the top cover of the hive, I was excited about this prospect, and couldn't wait to get home to learn what I needed to do to apply for a "Beekeepers Tobacco Permit." So, as I sat in a class at school and should have been concentrating on every word the teacher said, instead I was dreaming about my bees. That's when it happened.

It was early afternoon when my daydreaming was interrupted by the piercing sounds of air raid sirens. Suddenly, everyone bolted upright in their seats. As the teacher shouted for us to crawl under our desks for cover, we heard the eerie whistling sound of bombs screaming earthward. All around us was the cacophony of roaring airplane engines, exploding bombs, and the rattle of heavy-caliber machine guns. Through it all came the wail of the sirens. Although I was terrified, at the same time I was curious to see what was happening. On all fours I crawled over the hardwood floor through the exit and into the schoolyard. There I witnessed the sky filled with aircraft. German fighter planes were attacking hundreds of four-engine bombers on the way to the German heartland. The defense by Allied fighter planes was fast and furious. One moment they were corkscrewing upwards and another moment they were diving. Sometimes one of the planes would go into a steep dive and then rise straight up as it tried to get a tactical advantage on another aircraft. The success of the maneuver depended a great deal on the skill of the fighter pilot. I laid on my back against the wall of the school building watching the action with fear and awe. I was fascinated with airplanes and had studied the different types of planes used in war. I watched as a Messerschmitt desperately tried to outmaneuver a pursuing P-38. With guns spewing hundreds of 50-caliber bullets together with 20 mm shells from its wing cannon. The Messerschmitt was in a near-vertical dive, blazing away with all four machine guns. It looked as if both aircraft might slam into the school in another second or two. In addition, heavy-caliber machine gun bullets kicked up gravel in the schoolyard not far from me. A huge bomber corkscrewed toward earth in a screaming death dive, as crew members tumbled out of the fatally-stricken craft. Not all of the parachutes opened. I jumped involuntarily as one uniformed body slammed into pastureland adjoining the school grounds. The Messerschmitt made one final, desperate effort to climb steeply away from the devastating firepower of the P-38. A moment later, it exploded into a fireball and crashed straight down. At that moment I could see the smoke rising from several crash sites.

As quickly as it had started, it was over. Instant death and destruction had loomed so near. Now Drachten returned to life again and I shakily walked into the classroom just as students crawled out from underneath their desks. After school, I walked a short distance to the railroad station and boarded the tram on its way to a stop in Opende. The big locomotive pulling the cars barely left the station when it came to an unscheduled stop. I noticed German guards on both sides of the track. No one was allowed to exit the train. Nearly two hours passed before the wreckage of a crashed Messerschmitt was cleared and the train once again began moving toward its first regular stop, Opende.

It was not easy to get my mind off the dramatic events of the school day. Watching someone fall from the sky and smack into the ground to an instant death was more than a young boy can find peace with. Though I didn't talk about it, this incident was constantly on my mind as I helped Dad milk the cows, feed the calves, the pigs and the chickens. It wasn't until much later in the evening, while studying my school assignments for the following day, that I remembered my bees and the anticipated clandestine tobacco business. I found the application in among my "bee papers." The reason beekeepers were entitled to a tobacco allotment during the war was because the only way the beekeeper could harvest honey without getting killed by bee-stings was to tranquilize them with real tobacco smoke. It was about ten days later when a package arrived from Douwe-Egberts Tobacco Company. The package contained two pounds of real pipe tobacco. It was a little coarser than cigarette tobacco, but given that the kids smoked all kinds of dried leaves that didn't even resemble tobacco, my being able to get some of real tobacco would be regarded as a miracle. Before the tobacco had arrived, I contacted an elderly beekeeper, Mr. Loonstra, about the kind of pipe I would need. He gave me a short demonstration. The cup of the pipe was covered by what could be described as a small chimney. The beekeeper blew into the chimney by directing the pipe mouthpiece at the bees. How ingenious, I thought. I had been worrying about having to smoke a pipe. Now I learned that I wouldn't even get smoke in my mouth much less my lungs.

Mr. Loonstra was a kind old man with years of experience in taking care of bees and harvesting honey. I must have asked him endless questions. He promised that I could even use his centrifuge for extracting the honey from the cells where the bees had put the honey. After each cell was filled the bees would cover the small storage cell with a thin film of beeswax. Each frame contained hundreds of cells. I asked Mr. Loonstra what he used the honey for. "Well," he said, "the family uses a few jars but I sell most of it to neighbors and some to grocery stores. You'll get a lot more honey than your family can use too, Sietze. You won't have any problem selling your honey." This was very exciting. Not only would I get into the tobacco business, but I would also be able to earn a little money selling honey.

At school during the lunch break I talked to a number of kids and told them that I would have real tobacco which I could sell in small packages. They wanted to know how many cigarettes they could make and what the price would be. I told them that I would include a package of cigarette paper which they were accustomed to using when they rolled their own junk-filled cigarettes. Then I told them if they rolled their cigarettes thin they would be able to make ten maybe fifteen thin cigarettes and the price would be fifty cents including a package of the proper paper leafs for making their own smokes. They wanted to place orders for two or more little bags of my tobacco but I told them that I would only sell one small bag per person. The news spread like wildfire and before the day was over I had orders for twenty-two little bags of tobacco. I was a little worried when I stopped at a small shop for some small paper bags. They were only ten cents for a dozen but I didn't want to get rid of too much of my tobacco. At home, for my own information, I rolled a thin cigarette. Then I removed the paper foil surrounding the tobacco and placed it on a small saucer. Okay, I needed about fifteen times that quantity in each little bag. I knew that, as a beekeeper, I would be allotted an additional quantity of tobacco later. Interestingly, my parents never knew that their young teenaged son was a "black market" tobacco dealer.

By the early spring of 1945 we knew the Germans were on the ropes. The occupying forces also knew it. But instead of relieving their yoke of oppression, the Germans became more bitter and brutal. Life became very dangerous for many including our family. Mom and Dad had been active in the underground resistance movement and I knew that we were hiding a man who was wanted dead or alive by the Germans. If he were found our whole family would be executed. Dad looked very serious when he walked up to me. "Sietze, we suspect that you know about our secret radio," Dad said, looking at me as if expecting an answer.

Almost imperceptibly, I nodded.

"But we don't think you know about our secret pistol."

Fortunately, he didn't seem to expect an answer. I didn't need to confess that I knew about the pistol and where its secret hiding place was. I also knew that Mr. Schipper, the man we were hiding, had a pistol that was much larger than the one hidden just below the roof tiles in the straw. Mr. Schipper was a police officer in a city in the province of Friesland. He was deeply involved in the Dutch resistance movement but had managed to escape when his group was caught recovering weapons dropped by the British to equip the Dutch freedom fighters.

"It's getting much too dangerous to keep those items," Dad continued. "If I were to be captured, the Germans would ask me about such things. If I was to deny it, and the items should subsequently be found, they would kill me on the spot. That's why we want you to take the radio and the gun and bury them somewhere. Make sure it's not an obvious place that could be easily discovered. Instead you must find a very good place to hide these items. Mom and I do not want to know where you hid them, and you are absolutely never to breathe a word about their existence."

With that he reached into his inside coat pocket and handed me the revolver and a small box of bullets. As both my parents turned to go into the house, Mom looked at me and said: "You know where the radio is, don't you, Sietze?" I nodded remembering the many times I had seen my mother crawling in the space under an alcove bed to listen to the Dutch language message for the Dutch underground, broadcast by the BBC from London. What I did not know was that we would soon experience the most dramatic and life-threatening day of the entire five years of Nazi occupation. The details of my experiences during those five years are described in my book, *The Way it Was.*

New beginnings

The day of liberation came in early May 1945. With shovel in hand I headed for the chicken coop. I moved the heavy drinking water container and started digging to unearth the carton containing the old radio I had buried a few months earlier. Since I had not taken much time to complete that secret operation, I knew it wasn't very deep. Because I didn't want to damage the old radio, I was digging carefully. A plan had already been forming in my mind about how to reuse it. Suddenly I saw a big mouse with a family of small mice jump through the hole I had just put in the cardboard box. Somehow a pregnant mouse had chewed her way through the cardboard, built a cozy nest inside and was busy raising her family. After

I had removed the cardboard box containing the radio, I filled the hole and shoved the chicken water feeder back in place. That's when I finally turned my attention to the old radio. I didn't have the luxury of time when I had buried it and the old wooden radio didn't have a back cover. Nor did I have an electrical outlet nearby to see if it still worked. Instead I told my parents that the old radio had housed a mouse family and I didn't think it would ever work again. "Can I have it?," I asked. Since liberation had finally come they were in a good mood and agreed that I could have the old radio.

My interest in the mysteries of electronics was awakened when, as a little boy, I was visiting my grandpa and grandma Hoekstra. Grandma always fixed me a cup of tea with a large cube of sugar and a cookie. Grandpa got up and turned a switch on a little wooden box with a fabric grille hanging on the wall in their living room. Suddenly the voice of a man emanated from the box. I stared at the box and wondered how a human voice could come from something that was clearly too small to accommodate even the tiniest human being. Later, after the war began, I remember sitting in church listening to the sounds of airplane engines. I knew that pilots in those planes were able to communicate with other airplanes as well as controllers in a tower on the ground. Those were the mysteries that fascinated me. What I could not have known was that those experiences would later lead to what would be a big part of my career.

But on that day in 1945, I became the owner of an old radio. After housing a family of mice, I wasn't at all surprised that the radio no longer worked. Maybe I could learn how to fix it. As a fifteen-year-old boy I didn't know that I couldn't start a small radio business. In my imagination nothing was impossible. My search for information about electronics had started. Then in late 1945 I read an announcement about a new publication called Electron. I wasted no time ordering a subscription. It was exciting when, after a long wait, the mailman, Mr. Dalmolen, delivered the first issue to our house. Not only did I read every word of all the articles, but also the advertisements. After the end of the Second World War new radios were not available for nearly a year. The Dutch manufacturers of radios such as NV Philips, as well as all the German electronics manufacturers, had all been required to manufacture electronics for the German military. That, I thought, was the reason I found so many want ads in my first copy of Electron magazine inquiring about purchasing radio parts. That gave me an idea. I had an old radio that didn't work but was full of parts.

I befriended a young man living in an adjoining town who also had an interest in all things "electronic." His last name was Veenstra and before long we established a little company and named it "Radio Veenron." We placed a small ad in Electron magazine offering radio parts for sale. Our customers wouldn't know that we were just a couple of teenagers and that our business was conducted from my family farmhouse. I quickly needed to learn the difference between a radio power transformer and a filter condenser and everything in between. I received orders and mailed the parts to the customers who lived a long way from my hometown, Opende. Not even my parents knew about my business activities. However, that all soon changed.

The weather was pleasant one early morning in the province of Zeeland. It was a province located in the most Southwestern corner of Holland near Belgium and the North Sea. Two men with a common interest in radios and electronics had read the small "Radio Veenron" ad. Since radio parts were scarce after the war, they decided to make the long drive from Zeeland to the province of Groningen, which was located in the extreme Northern part of Holland. I can only imagine that, upon their arrival in the small town of Opende, they breathed a sigh of relief. They had been driving for several hours in an old car that somehow had survived being requisitioned by the Germans during the war. I can imagine that they drove slowly along the brick main street of Opende looking for storefronts. Especially a storefront emblazoned with "Radio Veenron" on the large display window. They must have eventually come to the conclusion that there was no such store. I can imagine that one of the gentlemen pulled his copy of the magazine from his pocket to check the ad and the company address. Yes, there it was, Radio Veenron, D219 Opende, Gron.

Because it was late in the afternoon, they must have started by asking for directions. Finally they took the sand path and arrived at our farmhouse where my parents, my siblings and I all lived. Fortunately, I was attending a school specializing in agriculture and not home. My mother was no less surprised than the two gentlemen from Zeeland. However my mom knew nothing about it. I don't think she told the completely flabbergasted gentlemen that her son might know more about it. After I arrived home from school I had a lot of questions to answer together with an order to "cease and desist." That was the end of our Radio Veenron enterprise but not the end of my interest in radio and electronics. That continued until the day our family immigrated to the United States in May 1948.

CHAPTER THREE

LEARN FROM YOUR MISTAKES

DON'T BE AFRAID OF MID-STREAM ADJUSTMENTS

I've known Sid for twenty-five years and worked for him the last thirteen. Prior to working for Exxel Pacific, I owned my own floor covering business. After losing that business I hit a low like never before. I had lost everything, I mean everything. Worse yet I lost my confidence, reputation and integrity. I took it so personally that I physically got sick. Sid and his partner heard about my troubles and gave me an opportunity to put together an in-house interior program unlike anything offered by other general contractors. That department has since become very successful.

During the entire process of losing my business and then taking the new position, Sid spoke such positive words. He cheered me on when nobody else did. He's such a great person to have in your life. People who want to be a success need mentors that come alongside them who truly care about them. That is what Sid is all about, he has such high integrity and character. He's worked very hard, is very honest and is someone you like to follow.

Personally, prior to my partner passing away from cancer after a long illness, Sid was a very powerful influence on her as well. He called her every day to cheer her up and share jokes. As my partner's caregiver I learned early on that I couldn't do things alone because it was so overwhelming. I am convinced that his friendship helped her to live longer than the doctors predicted. After she passed away Sid kept in touch regularly and helped me get through the grief.

Knowing Sid has made me a better person. Having him as a friend and mentor has meant so much to me.

—Mike Kussman has been in the floor covering business for much of his life. He is nearing retirement but still works in the floor covering department of Exxel Pacific Construction.

Helping others to achieve the best they can in spite of mistakes along the way

When you make mistakes, do you admit your errors and move forward or do you stew about it? During my career I have founded many businesses and made tons of mistakes along the way. Rather than stew about them, I have learned from them and moved on. Much of what I've learned came from the inspiring words of great people who have similarly learned how to benefit from their missteps.

Starting Life Anew in America

The first year and a half after arriving in America I helped my dad with farm work. He was a little over fifty years old and it wasn't easy for him to get started all over again in a new country. I'm sure they had not expected an easy life but neither had they expected living and working in a cruel paradise. It would be many years later that author Hylke Speerstra would write a book about early experiences of Dutch immigrants entitled *Cruel Paradise.*

Less than two months after arriving in America I met a nice young lady whose name was Margaret Tjoelker. Neither of us could have imagined that more than sixty years later we would still be both happily married and also best friends. Less than two years after meeting Margaret, who worked as a teller in a local bank, we were married. We were only nineteen years old at the time. Except for the dollar bill I earned on the ship, I was penniless. Needless to say, my dad was not happy that he no longer would have his oldest son helping him get established in farming again. Margaret's father was also a farmer and owned a sizeable dairy farm. He had acquired a small farm and home nearby, which he rented to us after we married. What he did not know at the time was that farming wasn't in my blood. But because I had no money, I had no choice. The first ten years of our marriage I was a small dairy farmer. I decided to make the best of it while, at the same time, dreaming about starting a little business on the side.

"What are you reading honey?" asked Margaret. We had just finished our evening meal and I was paging through a magazine. "Well sweetheart, let me explain" I responded. "You know I'm really interested in electronics and I read that I could study to become a radio and TV technician by ordering a mail order course from DeVry Technical Institute." The course included textbooks, tests and electronic parts to build my own radio and even a small transmitter.

"Isn't that too expensive?" Margaret asked. "Yes Hon," I answered, "that's the problem. You're expecting our first child and you won't be able to continue to work at the bank. Our little farm with twelve cows doesn't produce enough milk to make a living. I just have to make some extra money before I can even think about ordering the electronics course. Don't worry honey. I'll think of something. I know it's my job to make a living and somehow I will. I don't want you to have to worry about it."

Margaret got up and came around the table to plant a little kiss on my forehead. "I know you will honey. Despite what our parents might think, I know you're not dumb and lazy."

Because Margaret didn't like to drive when the roads were snowy and slippery, I used her 1937 Chevrolet to take her to the bank and pick her up in the evening. It was early 1950 and the winter weather that year in Whatcom County was the most brutal winter ever recorded. This was prior to the age of computers and before bank employees could leave work before all the day's transactions were balanced. As a result, I often had to wait for her outside in her car. I never waited for her in the bank because I didn't want to be seen there. I felt like a bum whose wife was earning a living for the family. While waiting for her one day

I wandered into a nearby drug store to look at their magazine rack. One magazine titled "Salesmen Opportunity" captured my attention. As I began to page through it I felt in my pocket and found a quarter to purchase the fifteen-cent magazine.

That evening, after dinner, I devoured that magazine. By this time I was tired of thinking about myself as being a bum. I decided to become a door-to-door salesman selling "automatic floor waxers." Remember, this was 1950 when most floors were linoleum which, at the time, required the person doing the household cleaning to get on their hands and knees to apply a coat of wax to the floors. The automatic floor waxers I would be selling consisted of a broom-like handle attached to a replaceable soft mop head connected to wax container can which was activated by a trigger line. With the floor waxer all the operator had to do was fill the can with their favorite wax solution, pull the trigger and move the broom-like waxer back and forth over the linoleum. No more hands and knees scrubbing and the unit only cost the housekeeper $4.95. If I ordered a dozen from the factory my cost would be just under $2.50 each. The problem was that I didn't have the money to order a dozen. To raise the money I got a job using a shovel and axe to cut into the frozen ground and expose broken water pipe for a neighboring farmer. The work was truly backbreaking for an hourly pay of only 75 cents. It took me a week to get the thirty dollars I needed to order a dozen automatic floor waxers.

Before calling on prospective customers, Margaret thought I should try to make myself look a little older. After all, at the time I was only nineteen. We bought a brown felt hat normally worn by well-dressed gentlemen. Armed with a new hat and dressed in my only suit I was ready to hit the road. After making several calls I had only sold one floor waxer. It beat the 75-cents-an-hour job but I was not yet what I would consider a good salesman. Something was wrong with my presentation. I decided to change it. Rather than carrying the waxer to the prospect's home and asking if they were interested in buying one, instead I left the floor waxer in the car. When the lady or gentleman came to the door I would ask: "If I could show you how you can wax your linoleum without getting down on your hands and knees, would you be interested?"

Simply by analyzing my sales approach I learned a valuable lesson. The day before I had probably called on at least a dozen homes and made one sale. If I had tripled the number of stops and called on three dozen homes I might have sold three units. This would have made selling just a numbers game. Call on more homes, sell more waxers. By changing my approach and making the prospect curious before showing my product made my selling more efficient.

I never forgot the lesson I learned. It wasn't long after that I began to order the floor waxers in quantities of a gross (144) at a time and getting a 65 percent discount. I even sold the units to stores at a 40 percent discount if they bought a minimum of six units. But the most important lesson was that I learned how to be successful. It wasn't long before I was able to open a small savings account at the bank. In addition, I ordered the electronic technician course from DeVry Technical Institute. Now I was a farmer, a door-to-door salesman and a home study student.

CHAPTER FOUR

THERE IS NO FREE LUNCH

BOOTSTRAPPING, ANGELS AND OTHER CREATIVE METHODS VERSUS LOANS AND FINANCING

I got to know Sid while growing up through his son, Alan, who was a boyhood friend. After graduating from high school I decided not to go on to college and instead try my hand working in agriculture. That decision was based on my observation that not all people benefit from college and, in my case, I was better suited to learn on the job. After taking a couple jobs that lasted a few years, one day I received a letter from Sid offering me a position in a new company he was starting. To this day I keep that letter in my desk drawer. At the time I was twenty-five and married with two kids. Sid was proposing that I join his sons Alan and Jim in a telecommunications venture. The year was 1981 and it was just prior to the breakup of AT&T which led to the explosive growth in telecommunications. Sid had just sold his radio station and was looking to reinvest his money into something new and saw the impending breakup of AT&T as an opportunity.

At the time I didn't know anything about telecommunications. Over lunch I told Sid that while I had no knowledge, I was eager to learn. Over the next couple years I self taught myself how to build the installations side of what became Baron Communications. I'm a hands-on kinda guy from a large family and was comfortable learning how to install phone systems. Though Alan eventually left the business, Jim stayed on and took over the sales functions.

From the first days, Sid and I hit it off well. I think he valued my work ethic and I certainly respected his ability to build businesses. Rather than going into debt Sid believed in finding other more creative ways to fund his businesses. In this case he used the profits from the sale of the radio station for funding.

After five years Sid decided to expand the business and purchased a telecommunications company just north of Seattle. This was the first of many such acquisitions as we grew the company from its base in Lynden to larger markets in the northwest corridor of Washington state.

In 1986, Jim Baron and I decided to purchase the company from Sid. Over the next eight years Jim and I bought eight other companies. Sid was involved in every one of the acquisitions even though he no longer owned the company. He is a master negotiator with an amazing winsome personality which he used to get the best deal. For Sid negotiating is all about overcoming obstacles. He gets a twinkle in his eye as he gets close to closing a deal.

Because Sid was a pilot we often flew together to meet with the heads of the companies we acquired. It was during those trips that Sid taught me about debt strategies, value propositions, mitigating risks, and how to interpret profit and loss statements. Sid never risks what he cannot afford to lose and knows how to find the win-win in every deal he makes.

To this day Sid and I maintain a lunch relationship. He remains a valuable friend and mentor. One time over lunch I told Sid that I was considering offering leasing to our customers. Within hours he sent me the forms and and lease agreements we still use to this day. He was instrumental in helping us to bootstrap the leasing business and it has since grown to over two million dollars in lease holdings. And it all started over a lunch with Sid.

—Phil Bratt, is the CEO of Baron Telecommunications with their home office located in Bellingham, WA.

Bootstrapping vs Borrowed Capital

According to a recent article in *Inc.* magazine, a new way many entrepreneurs are funding their fledgling businesses is through credit card dept. Problem is, if you can't pay off your cards when they come due you risk paying a hefty amount of interest. A key driver to success is keeping costs down, especially interest fees on borrowed capital. Better for you to take a second job than to pay those high interest costs.

If you require working capital during the startup phase, consider small investments from those who know you best, your friends and family. Even though it may feel awkward to ask others for help, it does provide you with an opportunity to show your business plan to others. It is amazing how many good ideas will come from the people who know you best. While some may invest, others won't be in a position to help or might be unsure of your idea.

How I Did It

As a successful salesman I felt that Margaret's old 1937 Chevy did not convey that image. Pride caused me to buy a newer car which we couldn't really afford yet. For the first time in my life I got a bank loan. Every month I worried that I wouldn't be able to make the \$68.50 monthly payment, and that month finally arrived. When it did, I walked nervously into the bank and asked to talk to the president of the bank. He was a big man with a friendly face. I said, nervously "Mr. LeCocque, I'm so sorry that I cannot make the total payment this month. I can only pay \$30.00 this month. But I think I can catch up in the next three months. Will that be OK?" Mr. LeCocque invited me into his private office and said "Sid, I wish all our customers were like you. They don't make their payments and we don't hear from them." Looking straight into my eyes he said, "I'm impressed. I appreciate you coming in and telling me. Now I know I will never need to worry about your car loan because you are worried about it."

CHAPTER FIVE

REPUTATION IS EVERYTHING:

DEALING WITH CUSTOMERS, VENDORS AND CO-WORKERS

One of the things I'm most impressed by in Sid is the way he interacts with others. It is something that is quite noticeable at the annual Exxel Pacific holiday party. Over the past several years the company has grown significantly especially since the addition of its second office in Seattle. What impresses me at these gatherings is the level of connection Sid has with all of the employees. There is such respect between Sid and the workers and vice versa. In many companies, as they grow, the founder becomes more irrelevant in the daily lives of the workers. This is definitely not the case at Exxel Pacific where Sid is both respected by and connected to the employees. Even though he is no longer as involved in day-to-day operations, I'm so impressed by how Sid keeps involved in the personal lives of everyone in the company. People just love the guy and he loves them back.

Often I stop by the office to pick Sid up for lunch. When we return to the office one feels the respect going both ways. It seems like there is no status, instead he sees the person rather than that person's position. Sid has taught me a lot in my own work as the CEO of an accounting firm. Rather than view myself as someone who is above those who work with me, instead I see being CEO as a servant role. It is not about status. When I show up at my office I try to take the same approach as Sid in that each person in our firm—from owner to the newest hire just starting out—is equal in terms of my time and attention. It allows me to bring passion every day while keeping humble. It is something I learned from watching Sid.

Over the years, as his accountant, I've had the great pleasure of meeting with Sid and Margaret in their home. Typically these meetings start with fifteen or twenty minutes of him asking me personal questions about myself, my family, and my role in my company. His questions are always very well thought out. As an accountant charging by the hour, I'm always conscious about time. Sid isn't. With him you never feel like you are on the clock. It is almost as if he has prepared for my visit and has a process he has thought deeply about. It has taught me a lot about the process of getting to know people and helped me tremendously in terms of my ability to connect with clients and the people at our firm.

When I'm having lunch with someone, for example a partner who I know is building a house, I start out by

> asking about their house, their children, or about their hobby before getting into the topic of our meeting. The same with clients. I might ask about their grandchildren or their most recent vacation or about what's going on in their business before getting into the various tax issues or estate planning or business accounting strategy. It is something I have learned from Sid. He has taught me a lot in that area.
>
> *—Marv Tjoelker, Certified Public Accountant, Partner / CEO, Larson Gross and Associates*

It's all about the Golden Rule

In the early 1950s I married a wonderful young lady. I was a small farmer with a passion for building a successful business. Both my father and father-in-law were farmers. It was the only way they knew how to make a living. My father-in-law acquired a small farm and helped me buy some cows. However, farming wasn't in my blood. I knew that it was now my responsibility to make a living for my family and was determined to provide for my wife and our young son. I would not fail them. It was my hope that the farm would produce sufficient income to pay our monthly living expenses and my sideline door-to-door selling activities would help me save some money to grow the business. I had no intentions of making direct selling my lifelong career. It would merely be a stepping stone for greater accomplishments.

In the evenings I studied my DeVry Technical Institute electronics course material. I completed all the assignments, submitted the tests and within two years received an impressive looking diploma. I was now qualified as a radio-TV technician. However, I had never worked in an electronic repair shop and had no job experience. I did have enough self-confidence to believe I could learn on my own. At around the same time, Margaret and I purchased a piece of needed furniture from a small local furniture store. The owner's name was Joe and he agreed to sell us the furniture on credit if we made regular monthly payments. We never missed a payment even if it was only ten dollars a month. Over time we came to know Joe well and he, in turn, knew he could trust us. After completing my technical course I walked into his store one afternoon and started a conversation. "Joe, you don't sell television sets do you?" I asked. He responded that he did not but that his wholesaler had encouraged him to stock a few Coronado TV sets. But because he knew they required service along with the installation of a roof mounted antenna (and that he didn't know anything about TV), Joe decided against stocking them. I told him his decision was certainly understandable.

I went on to inform Joe that I was interested in selling, installing and servicing televisions. If he agreed to pay me a commission whenever I sold a TV set, I would be happy to take the position. Joe leaned against his store service counter. He looked thoughtful and somewhat surprised as he looked at me. "Sid I know you're farming. I didn't know you knew anything about TV." I explained that I had recently completed a home study course in servicing radio and TV sets and would love to have an opportunity to get started. Joe kindly agreed to fix up a little shop in the back of his store that I could use as a radio-TV repair shop. He would also order two or three Coronado TVs for display in the store and pay me ten percent commission when I made a sale. That was my start in the electronics business. Now I had the opportunity to put my book learning to the test with some practical experience.

One day, I walked into a radio-TV shop only one block from where my little shop was located. The owner's name was Frank and he was busy working on the chassis circuitry of a television. I noticed an older console TV with a round picture tube about thirteen inches in diameter. "Frank, that's a pretty old set isn't it?" "Yes," he replied, "I worked on that old thing for hours and it's beyond repair. The owner finally traded it in. You can have it if you get that piece of junk out of my way." Frank didn't know that I would soon be a competitor with a repair shop only one block away. I took the old set and was delighted that I would finally have an opportunity to get some practical experience attempting to fix an old TV that, according to Frank, was beyond repair. I looked for the model number of the old GE black and white television set. Remember, this was several years before color TV became a reality. I ordered a schematic diagram for the set, removed the chassis and placed it upside down on my new workbench to expose the circuitry. Then I took my DeVry Technical Institute multi-meter and began checking the voltages at the contacts for the various vacuum tubes and comparing the voltage readings with those indicated on the schematic. It wasn't long before I discovered that the where the diagram indicated 190 volts should be at the plate terminal of the tube was instead registering zero voltage.

That could only be caused by a burned out resistor. I replaced the resistor and—bingo—the set was fixed. It only required a fifteen-cent part and a half hour of my time. I literally jumped with joy and was extremely proud of myself.

I should have realized that to walk into Frank's shop boasting about repairing the TV set he had slaved over for hours would trample on his self-esteem. Using some colorful language he told me where the door was. I have regretted that ever since and should have known that it was neither kind nor appropriate. I was simply blinded by my elation to have succeeded so quickly on my first project as a TV technician. Especially after a man with years of experience had given up on it.

It wasn't long before I sold my first television set. Now I needed to buy an antenna, a chimney mounting bracket, lead-in wire and everything else necessary to produce a picture on a new TV set. In order to purchase the parts I needed to go to Waitkus Supply, a wholesale distributor in Bellingham, and try to open an account. The owner's name was Stan and I asked to talk to him.

After introducing myself he said "Oh, yes, Sid. I heard about you opening a little shop in the back of a store in Lynden." I hoped he hadn't heard about me from Frank who had probably been a customer for years. His smile put me at ease and we struck a deal. Perhaps someone had told him that he could trust me, I thought while driving my green Studebaker pick-up back to the shop. The truck was loaded with everything I needed to start installing TV antennas along with some small parts and radio and TV tubes. (It was way before the use of transistors and solid state electronics) Stan had given me an invoice for over 300 dollars and I promised to pay his company regularly. At that time, stocking small quantities of TV antennas and supplies wasn't something I could afford to do. Instead I made frequent trips to Bellingham to get what I needed and avoid getting into financial overload. At times I would pick up Margaret and our little boy to accompany me to Bellingham. We would stop at the take-out window of a fast food place, buy a nineteen-cent hamburger and a small milkshake. Then we'd drive to a park and enjoy our lunch and each other's company. Taking time out to spend with the family is something I've always believed in. Good relationships start at home.

CHAPTER SIX

KNOW YOUR RISKS:

NEVER LET YOUR HOPES AND DREAMS PUT YOU IN JEOPARDY

Like Sid, I also immigrated to America from the Netherlands. At the time, I was twenty-six years old and had worked as a trader on the Amsterdam Stock Exchange. My decision to immigrate was a very difficult one. The year was 1956 and The Relief Act which allowed immigration that was hassle free from Europe, was ending. Earlier I had met my future wife Julie whose father, Ed Douma, was the head basketball coach of Calvin College in Grand Rapids, Michigan.

I arrived in Grand Rapids on December 6, 1956 and married Julia the following year. In 1959 we moved across the country to Bellingham, Washington where I met Sid who had recently started Motivating Sounds which offered background music primarily to businesses. I decided to invest in the company and also set up its bookkeeping system.

From day one I trusted Sid and in all our years working together never had a written contract. Everything was done with a gentleman's agreement. Ours was a relationship based on mutual respect. Mind you, we didn't always agree but we worked things out. We had a lot of ups and downs but overall it was fantastic. To this day we still meet for lunch once a month and hope to continue getting together for many more years to come.

From the beginning Sid and I have bounced ideas off each other and enjoyed our brainstorming sessions. We analyzed everything and knew how to measure risks. Sid would have made a great judge because he would not take too much or give too much up. He is a straight shooter. Sid is also good at listening to all sides before making a decision.

During the early days at Motivating Sounds our backs were against the wall financially. I even offered to take on a part-time job to help but Sid wanted no part of it. Instead we both decided to work even harder to bring in more background music business. No matter what the circumstances, we always opened each day for business with a positive attitude. I remember one cold winter morning as we stood warming ourselves by the furnace telling Sid that he would one day be wealthy because the radio station he owned in the same building would be worth a lot of money some day. He looked at me in bewilderment as if he didn't believe what I was saying—but I was right about it.

> Working with Sid has been a beautiful ride filled with hard work and excitement. Though we took a few chances, we never took risks we couldn't afford.
>
> *—Rook VanHalm owned and managed the Lynden Travel Agency. He has been a long time partner of the author and they remain best friends. He is retired and resides in Bellingham, WA.*

Expanding

After opening my TV repair business, something had to give. I decided to discontinue my direct-selling activities. Having to milk eighteen cows every morning and every evening on top of everything else was more than I could handle. Especially since I had to dress like a businessman every morning and drive to my shop in Lynden which was about eighteen miles from our farm. In the early evening I would come home, quickly put on my white coveralls over my suit and milk my cows. Then we would sit down for dinner. Quite often after dinner I would still have to make a service call to repair a customer's TV set. At that time televisions were large pieces of furniture with a heavy chassis, a glass cathode ray picture tube and were, as a result, simply too heavy for a customer to bring in to the shop.

One evening during dinner Margaret said, "I talked to my cousin Lawrence today. He knows you have a small shop in the back of Joe's store and thought you might be interested expanding." I was all ears and asked what he had in mind. Margaret explained that Lawrence owned a small retail store in downtown Lynden with half of the space rented to a jewelry store and the other half sitting vacant. It turned out he wanted to offer it to me to rent. I was speechless. Imagine a storefront with a display window facing the sidewalk and retail space to display merchandise. The following day I called Lawrence and made an appointment to look at the space. It was a Saturday afternoon when I walked to the front door with Lawrence. He explained that there was a large area in the back of the store and that only a small portion was rented to a shoe repair shop. The rest of the back room space could be used as a spacious TV and radio repair shop. I was excited about the possibilities but didn't show that in any way. After all if I gave an indication of a positive impression it would put me in a weaker position to negotiate favorable rental terms. Lawrence explained that it would be a great way of expanding my business and it wouldn't cost me an arm and a leg. I asked him what the rent would be. He quoted me a monthly figure to which I responded, "Lawrence, thank you for showing me your space. I'm going to have to think about it."

"THE MAKING OF FRIENDS, WHO ARE REAL FRIENDS, IS THE BEST TOKEN WE HAVE OF A MAN'S SUCCESS IN LIFE."

EDWARD EVERETT HALE

Going from a little repair shop in the back of a furniture store to a downtown retail location would be a huge—nearly impossible—jump for someone who didn't have any capital.

How could I buy enough stock to fill a small retail store with a few TV sets, some radios and maybe a tape recorder or two? To do it I would have to contact a wholesale distributor based in Seattle. I headed for Seattle armed only with a list of references, which included the bank where I had my car loan. After checking my references, the distributor agreed to sell me a limited amount of inventory on credit. Since my farming still covered our monthly family expenses I was able to pay for the merchandise as it sold. This was often prior to the thirty days credit the supplier extended. Needless to say, my suppliers never had to worry about me paying my bills. Before long the wholesaler encouraged me to stock even more merchandise and said, "Baron, your credit rating is sky-high."

I was now a full-fledged merchant in downtown Lynden. The top of the store's display window was proudly adorned with the sign, "Baron's TV and Radio." It wasn't long before I needed help in repairing radios and TVs. Jake was a friend who had helped me to learn the Morse code which I needed in order to qualify for my amateur radio operator's license from the FCC. Jake had been mostly bedridden and not well for a number of years. As a result he had not been able to work. When the doctors finally determined that his problem was caused by his thyroid gland he was able to get the proper medication. Fortunately, he gradually improved. At the time he was in his late forties and had lost all hope of ever being employed again. It took some encouragement for Jake to give it a try. He would come in and help whenever he felt well and leave as his energy faded. Jake continued to be my friend and associate for at the next twenty-five years.

Less than two years later the small retail space was clearly inadequate for our growing business. At that time I had boundless energy and didn't worry about the stress from working too hard. I started each day milking my eighteen cows, ate breakfast and six days a week opened the store at nine o'clock. Almost every evening, after milking and doing the farm chores, I still had TV service calls to make. Expanding the store would likely make it feasible, financially, to hire an additional employee or two.

"THE ONLY WAY OF DISCOVERING THE LIMITS OF THE POSSIBLE IS TO VENTURE A LITTLE WAY PAST THEM ... INTO THE IMPOSSIBLE."

ARTHUR C. CLARKE

A larger building on the same block, which previously was a grocery store, had recently vacated. The owner lived in an apartment at the rear of the 5000-square-foot building which was too large for our business. I talked the owner into renting me half the space, which was many times larger than our current location. The owner, whose name was Herb, was a pleasant man with a wiry frame and an easy smile. "Herb," I said, during the course of our negotiations, "If my business keeps growing I may need the other half of your space." Herb smiled and said, "Sid, I think you'll do well here. I don't think anyone else is likely to rent the other half. Whenever you are ready, I'll give you a good deal."

It wasn't too long before we needed additional space and occupied the entire store. Now the store was filled with TV sets, stereo systems, radios, tape recorders and before long I added organs, pianos, guitars and band instruments. The business was really growing. Energy-wise, I was burning the candle at both ends. With an expanding business and growing family, something had to give. I brought on more employees at the store and hired a milker to take care of my morning and evening farm chores. Sundays the store was closed. It became our family day—which by then had expanded to Margaret and our four sons. Since my family was more important than anything else, Margaret and I decided to hire a babysitter for Saturday evenings so we could have a dinner date. It allowed us to spend a little time together and for me to fill her in on my business activities for the week. Margaret, in exchange, shared her child-rearing challenges with me. After attending church on Sunday, I devoted the rest of the day to playing with our young sons.

Increasingly I became aware of the relentless pressure of my activities and ever-increasing responsibilities. One Sunday morning, on our way back from church, Margaret and I both remember me saying, "Hon, I wish I could take a three-month vacation." She looked at me with an understanding expression indicating she knew what both of us knew. Any vacation was out of the question.

To help relieve the mounting pressure, I liked to plan elaborate pranks. Just a couple years ago someone rang the doorbell at our home. The middle aged gentleman smiled and,

HENRY FORD, WHO BELIEVED HE COULD DEVELOP A SYSTEM TO MASS PRODUCE AUTOMOBILES, PUT IT SIMPLY: "WHETHER YOU BELIEVE YOU CAN 'DO' A CERTAIN THING OR 'NOT'—YOU ARE RIGHT."

with a slight questioning inflection in his voice asked, "Sid?" Suddenly I recognized him and enthusiastically invited him in. Richard was a college student when I had hired him as a part-time technician in our service department. That was a lifetime ago. Now he was a business executive living with his wife and grown children in Minnesota. We reminisced for more than an hour and laughed at the hilarious prank I had pulled on him. Back then he was trying to repair a phonograph record changer mechanism. What he didn't know was that Jake and I had connected the mechanical device via a virtually invisible wire that, when Jake pushed a concealed button, would deliver about a 2000 volt charge to the mechanism. It was high voltage but low current assuring that the unexpected jolt would not be life threatening. Undeterred, Richard left to purchase a pair of heavy duty leather gloves and then stood on an old rubber tire figuring he was completely insulated before touching that mechanism again. Suddenly a mighty howl reverberated through the building as a solid bluish arc snapped right through his leather gloves. He practically flew out of the building. It was more than his intelligent and inquisitive mind was able to comprehend. I appreciated his coming to visit so many years later.

(The complete details of the above and many other pranks are described in my book *Just Laugh About It)*

CHAPTER SEVEN

LIVE A BALANCED LIFE:

HANDLING STRESS IS KEY TO YOUR HAPPINESS AND WELL-BEING

I know Sid on a different level than most since I serve Exxel Pacific as corporate pilot. Because Sid is a pilot he generally sits up front next to me. That has allowed us hundreds of hours of discussion covering all manner of topics from relationships, current events, our families and our faith. As a Seventh Day Adventist my faith differs in terms of doctrine from Sid's which is from the Dutch Reformed tradition. Because I'm interested in biblical study we have had some very interesting conversations. In fact, a while back I began packing my Bible in the seat behind me. However, no matter what my beliefs, Sid has always shown me complete respect—which is a tribute to the kind of man Sid is. He has accepted me and made me feel like a member of his family.

What is incredible about Sid and his partner Kevin are that they have been so respectful of my faith which does not allow me to work from midnight Friday to midnight Saturday. Few companies are so respectful of the religious beliefs of others that they allow schedules to change in spite of the hassle it causes.

The reason Exxel established their corporate fleet was out of respect for the families of their employees. Since many of their projects are located in distant states they felt it important to provide a way for employees to spend the maximum time with their families without having to drive a huge number of hours or wait for commercial flights. Both Sid and Kevin believe in providing their employees with the tools necessary to do their jobs most efficiently so that they can have a good quality of life.

Since establishing their corporate fleet, sales have tripled. The reason the company made the investment is that they want their people to be happy. It is one reason turnover is so low. Exxel believes that God comes first, people second and business last. It is why the company is so successful. By allowing its employees to live a balanced life everyone benefits—from the employee, the employee's family, company management and its customers and vendors.

My personal feeling about Sid is that he is a man who lives by his convictions. After learning he had MS over forty years ago, he has helped those around him to live a balanced life.

—Roger Coon, is a professional commercial pilot with thousands of hours of experience. He serves as the chief pilot for Exxel Pacific LLC.

Running a retail store specializing in electronic sales and service, operating a seven-days-a-week radio station plus milking dairy cows and operating a farm simply became too much. I didn't worry about keeping my sanity but I probably should have. Margaret helped with the bookkeeping as much as possible. But, after all, she was taking care of a household which had by this time had grown to six children. In 1963, baby JulieAnn joined sister KayeLynn and her four big brothers. We decided to purchase a home in Lynden just three blocks from our business. Then we sold the cows and rented the farm. I was a farmer no more! Finally I was able to concentrate exclusively on my business activities.

The radio station was fun. I enjoyed my personal involvement in a number of broadcasting activities. It would have been easy to simply imitate what competing radio stations in the area were doing. However, it is my nature to be creative while serving our audience in different and special ways. I started hosting a weekly nighttime call-in program featuring interviews with a different guest each week. These included politicians and others covering a wide range of topics. For instance, one episode was called, "Why Marriages Fail," which allowed listeners to call the station and participate in discussing their relationships.

Many families had emigrated from Holland during the late 1940s through the early 1950s and settled in our county (Whatcom) as well as adjoining Skagit county. Thousands of others settled over the border in Canada's British Columbia. Just twelve years prior I was one of them. I remembered very clearly the Dutch songs along with popular and sacred music. Eventually I started importing records from Holland and introduced a Monday evening program called "Music from Holland." It was a one hour program with the first half hour devoted to popular music and the second half hour to sacred. I was the disc jockey and Margaret always accompanied me to the station. Our two oldest sons, Jim and Gerald, were now old enough to be babysitters which allowed Margaret to catch up on some of the radio station's bookkeeping. As I had expected, because the program was targeted to a defined audience, it became an instant hit. The number of listeners continued to grow as information about the show spread among the Dutch immigrant community.

In our efforts to expand the services to our community of listeners, we began broadcasting a local church service. A little later we began providing play-by-play broadcasting of local basketball games. It helped that because there were two high schools in Lynden, the basketball games were fiercely competitive. Another special program that kept the station's telephones ringing was a fundraising program for a well-known charity. I remember an elderly gentlemen walking in with a large can full of change. "Here Sid," he said. "We've saved coins for years. Here they are." I could tell he wanted to say something confidentially to me. He put his head near my ear and whispered: "You're doing a wonderful thing and I want to say God bless you." I thanked him and felt humbly grateful.

Providing all those services resulted in making our advertising sales soar. Rather than take a bonus, I plowed the money back into expanding the reach of the station. Within a few years we acquired a more powerful transmitter and antenna system and were operating at the maximum allowable power of 100,000 watts. Knowing that my broadcasting venture, against long odds, had become successful gave me a great deal of personal satisfaction.

There were aspects of starting, building and operating a commercial radio station that I had overlooked. Within a short time my reputation as a successful businessperson became well-known. Especially in the business community throughout Whatcom County.

With notoriety came both positive and negative consequences. Negative, because I was a somewhat shy and private person. Radio listeners thought of me as a public radio personality of sorts yet didn't know that I was very comfortable talking through a microphone to an unseen audience. Nor did they know that speaking publicly in front of a group of people petrified me with fear. Yet it was positive to know that many, including some of my friends, wondered how this young immigrant fellow could achieve so much in such little time. They didn't know that Margaret and I didn't have any money for luxuries and barely enough for basic necessities. That was because I was still in the "business-building" mode and took home a very modest monthly salary. Luckily, Margaret was frugal. She trusted me to do the right thing. We were happy with our six lovely children and with each other. That was most important because happiness is something money cannot buy.

One effect of my new-found notoriety came when I was asked to head the annual Red Cross, county-wide, fundraising drive. I understood that success came with responsibilities, which I accepted. Now I needed to recruit volunteers who would solicit donations in specific areas. One evening, which had been designated to meet with the volunteers, I was required to give a motivational talk along with instructions on how to be successful in collecting donations for the Red Cross. I managed to get through the talk in spite of being extremely nervous. At that moment had someone told me that in the future I would frequently be a public speaker, I would not have believed them.

"HAPPINESS IS NOT ELATION, BUT IS MORE OF A GENERAL FEELING OF CONTENTMENT THAT HELPS YOU COPE WITH LIFE'S CHALLENGES."

CHRISTINA FRANK

It was my custom to meet with my radio advertising salesman, whose name was Barry, to plan the week's promotions. During one of those meetings Barry told me that for some time his accounts in Bellingham had asked if our radio station could provide them with background music. That peaked my curiosity. I asked him to tell me more about it. He told me that many businesses provided background music in their stores supplied by Muzak, a national company. The music, which was piped into their stores, came with a hefty monthly fee. Barry went on to say that since he sold advertising on KLYN, people knew we were in the music business and wondered if we could provide it to their businesses. As Barry spoke I was staring into space, deep in thought. He finally asked what I was thinking. Breaking my silence I told Barry that I was in favor of offering background music in Bellingham only if we could make it economically feasible. This would require the music origination equipment to be located in Bellingham since leasing telephone lines from Lynden to Bellingham would be cost prohibitive. Barry interrupted me saying that he had already gotten approval from the manager of the largest hotel in Bellingham to install tape playing equipment in the hotel's equipment room. We could then have the telephone company connect our music to our client businesses.

All the hotel wanted in return was some free advertising on KLYN.

Barry had thought of the idea and laid much of the groundwork. Now I needed to do some calculations to determine what kind of cash investment was required for purchasing tape recording and playback equipment with large sixteen-inch reels capable of automatically switching directions and playing music continually. Having such large reels would only require being changed every other day. I knew the equipment would be expensive and that we didn't have the financial resources purchase it. Barry interrupted me again. He had friends who had indicated their desire to invest in our business. He seemed confident that we could get the money we needed from investors.

At the end of our meeting I knew there would be much to think about. It humbled me to know that other people would

"WE ALL EXPERIENCE STRESS IN OUR LIVES AND WE ALL REACT DIFFERENTLY TO DIFFERENT TYPES OF STRESS OR STRESSFUL CONDITIONS. THE MORE WE UNDERSTAND HOW STRESS CAN AFFECT OUR HEALTH, THE MORE WE NEED TO TAKE SUCH ACTION AS IS NECESSARY TO REDUCE STRESS."

SID BARON

have enough confidence in our company to trust me with their money. That night I didn't get much sleep. If I accepted money from others I was placing myself under obligation to make sure their money wasn't lost. I could live with losing some money early on but I could not live with losing other people's money. This time it wouldn't be a loan, which was subject to regular interest payments, but instead an investment. I would have to give them a certificate indicating that their investment, in fact, bought a small part of the company. This meant forming a corporation, which I had never thought about doing. I ordered a book from Prentice-Hall Publishers that, at the time, was considered the bible for starting corporations. It was a huge book which included numerous forms covering every aspect of the legal requirements governing corporations.

A few weeks later I had an attorney friend draft the Articles of Incorporation. The Bylaws were discussed and agreed to during our organizational meeting. With that, and a few mixed feelings, I had started another business. That was the birth of Motivating Sound, Inc.

With the infusion of a few thousand dollars in capital provided by investors, we were able to acquire the equipment to provide Motivating Sound background music to several businesses in Bellingham. Because the monthly fees were low, the number of customers we served were insufficient to cover our expenses. It was not a good start. I also hired an additional employee to help with bookkeeping and sales. The new employee was a tall, handsome man with deep brown eyes and pitch black hair. Born and raised in Amsterdam, he told me that when he was born his dad noticed his pitch black hair and called him "Rook," which is a member of the black crow family. That nickname stuck. Rook was a responsible, honest, and hardworking young man. He later became a minority partner and our friendship continues to this day.

Back then I never missed reading the monthly electronics periodicals. Once we started our background music corporation, I paid particular attention to any information pertaining to the industry. A small but rapidly growing area of background music was known as "on premise." It had remained small because long playing tape systems were not yet available. Soon, a company in New York began importing on-premise background music units with long-play, pre-recorded music cartridges on a continuous loop. They were known as

Möbius loop tapes and repeated every hour. While it was not a problem for the store's customers, it was a little annoying to their staff. I contacted the importer and indicated that our company would be interested in an exclusive franchise. Before long a representative of the importer called to set up a meeting. We met at Boeing Field in Seattle. My Piper Tri-Pacer came in very handy for that short flight. I learned from Mr. Ehrenzweig that his company, Jay Electronics, located in New York had the exclusive sales rights for the United States and Canada. I signed an agreement whereby Motivating Sound Inc., became the exclusive distributor of the Möbius on-premise background music system for the state of Washington and British Columbia in Canada. I was also required to sign a purchase order for one gross (144) background music units. Mr. Ehrenzweig agreed to 30-60-90 day payment terms on the first shipment. I knew we didn't have adequate capital. This put us under a huge amount of pressure to sell them. Most of that pressure I placed on myself. We soon hired two types of sales reps. One to establish dealers throughout our state and the other to sell the systems directly to customers. Because I was increasingly involved in managing our growing corporation, there was little time for me to concentrate on selling my retail store merchandise.

With the on-premise background music system we were on the leading edge of a new and growing industry. We established an office in Vancouver, B.C. and succeeded in setting up a distribution program for the province. I learned that when starting a new business in a relatively new industry not to expect anything to go easily nor smoothly. There are always numerous situations that develop that need to be dealt with expeditiously. When you employ sales representatives to sell new systems and they have no previous experience, you can expect to spend much time on the phone training them. After that first difficult year, Motivating Sound Inc. had sold several hundred on-premise background music systems and was reasonably successful.

However, during the second year serious problems surfaced. It was the 1960s and the electronic industry was beginning to transition from vacuum tubes to transistor technology. Unfortunately, our background music units used vacuum tubes which generate heat and the tape transport mechanism used a rubber belt from the electric motor to the tape drive pulley. We discovered that the material used in the rubber belt could not withstand the heat generated by the tubes for more than fourteen months. This resulted in our clients having to pack-up their unit and ship it back to our service department at no charge for repair work. This turned out to be an expensive problem that would be unsustainable for any length of time. I cancelled our contract with Jay Electronics and consulted with one our technical wizards who assured me that he could design a good "solid state" amplifier which used transistors instead of tubes. I knew that a U.S. Company, Viking Electronics, was building a cassette tape mechanism that didn't need a belt to transfer energy from the motor to the tape drive system. Soon Motivating Sound began to manufacture background music units of our own design. These units turned out to be far superior to the outdated tube units. To produce the units, we expanded our existing service department extensively and hired people to assemble, test and pack our Motivating Sound background music units. This included the assembly of the large cartridge tapes that played for eight hours before repeating. Subsequently we added an additional product line, which originated because of requests from some of our grocery store customers, to add a feature that would periodically announce specials with the sound coming from a small loudspeaker hidden on the store shelf amid the products to be promoted. We called it the "Modern Merchandiser," which was a unique system.

After a successful initial test we were strongly advised by our suppliers to go national. One factory representative offered to have us join them in their booth at the annual Consumer Electronics Show in Chicago in an attempt to sign up factory reps. I spent four days there, endlessly explaining and demonstrating our Modern Merchandiser to factory sales representatives from throughout the country. Many gave me their business cards and requested that we contact them at their place of business. That required us to hire someone who could travel around the country calling on those contacts. My traveling was out of the question due to my schedule, so instead I would have to find someone who possessed the skills to effectively make sales and be willing to drive all over the U.S. It was a tall order, but we did succeed in hiring a person I knew who had all the right ideas and abilities we needed.

The man we hired lived in Portland, Oregon. His name was Bill and he was a good-looking gentleman with a solid build. I visited him in his home where he lived with his wife. He was in his mid-forties, jet black hair, brown eyes and a friendly smile. He made a great first impression. His assignment was calling on the contacts I had made while in Chicago. His job was to sign up companies who agreed to sell our products. For myself, I was excited about the possibilities for expanding our company into the manufacture of electronic equipment and marketing in both the U.S. and Canada.

While I could visualize unlimited opportunities, my elation was tempered by the fear of failure. After all, we were still in bootstrapping mode which required us to self-fund any new ventures. We held a Motivating Sound Inc. corporate meeting in order to let the board

"NOTHING IN YOUR BUSINESS IS MORE IMPORTANT THAN YOUR REPUTATION. A GOOD REPUTATION IS UNQUESTIONABLY ONE OF THE BUSINESS OWNER'S MOST TANGIBLE AND MARKETABLE ASSETS. YOU CAN'T SIMPLY BUY A GOOD REPUTATION, YOU CANNOT BUY TRUST. IT IS SOMETHING THAT YOU EARN BY HONORING YOUR PROMISES. IT'S IMPORTANT TO COMMUNICATE WITH YOUR PARTNERS OR INVESTORS YOUR HONEST ASSESSMENT OF THE COMPANY. IT'S ESPECIALLY IMPORTANT TO DISCLOSE POSSIBLE PERILS THAT YOU ENVISION WHICH MIGHT PUT THEIR INVESTMENTS AT RISK."

SID BARON

know that if we began receiving substantial orders we were undercapitalized to expand our manufacturing facilities, our staff and our inventory. Because my efforts to obtain additional financing were unsuccessful, to survive required us to operate with the expectation that our dealers would pay their invoices promptly. Without that cash flow we would not be able to fulfill our obligations and could easily fail resulting in the loss of our investors' money.

After the meeting the stockholders expressed their appreciation at being informed about the condition of the company and for my candor. They told me not to worry about the money they invested and that they trusted me completely. That night I went home and fell into bed. As I prayed for peaceful slumber my mind raced in a thousand different directions—searching, hoping, and praying for some miracle that would make it possible for the company to survive and become successful. I had not yet fully learned that a mind under stress does not function well. As a pilot I had learned to treat stress with a calm, confident composure and never to panic because panic leads to disaster. But instead of sleeping soundly, I woke up drenched in perspiration.

The next morning at work, Linda, our secretary, called on the intercom: "Sid, Bill on the phone from Dallas, Texas. Line three."

I picked up the receiver. Bill needed me to come to Dallas and make some calls with our factory representatives to help them close a sale with a large grocery chain interested in the on-premise Modern Merchandiser system.

It was a very hot day when I arrived in Dallas. The factory reps that I had talked to while promoting our Motivating Sound merchandise in Chicago, were picking me up. Being from Holland and now living in Washington State, I was not exactly used to hot weather. It had been a grueling hot day with temperatures reaching just over 100 degrees. After a two-hour sales call we got into our car, which was parked in a hot asphalt parking lot. It was like squeezing into a hot oven. But I survived. After two days I had a purchase order in my pocket for a dozen Modern Merchandiser units.

It always took a few minutes before the air-conditioning system in the car reduced the temperature to a comfortable level. I had spent the entire day making calls with two key people from the firm representing our company.

Early that evening my business associates and I drove to a fancy restaurant for a nice dinner. The two salesmen were in their mid-thirties and had territories that covered three states, including Texas. As a result, they were used to spending evenings in bars and restaurants. Their lives, as sales reps, involved traveling five days a week and spending weekends with their wives.

That night we were sitting in the restaurant lounge ordering our first round of drinks. The night before I had learned that it was the custom for each member of the party to order a round. This meant when it came my turn I was expected to order a round. It wasn't until after the third round of drinks that dinner was suggested.

Fortunately I've always had a strong dislike for the effects of alcohol. As soon as I began feeling a little woozy I stopped drinking. In order to be one of the boys, I had to do a little faking to stay sober. Whenever the others looked at me or asked me a question, I took a sip. However, when their attention turned to the game playing on the TV, I poured part of my drink onto the floor. Soon the puddle under my chair grew larger.

I was pretty familiar with the lifestyles, customs and morals of some traveling salesmen. It was well known that traveling businessmen had options. For that reason I wasn't too surprised when they asked if I wanted them to arrange for a sleeping companion for me. And, I have to say, I felt the devil's hot breath in my ear, but I declined.

It was just before midnight when I took the elevator to the fourteenth floor of a big Dallas hotel. It had been a long two days in the city and I was beyond being tired. I'd been away for a while and I was longing for the comforting arms of my wife.

In my briefcase was an order for sixteen of our electronic Modern Merchandiser units and it was the first order for the inventory we had acquired from the defunct Salem, Oregon factory. I tossed my briefcase on the bed, pulled off my jacket and tie and sank in the deep-cushioned chair.

During the previous week I had spent several days at the electronics show held at the huge McCormick Place in Chicago. My vision of building Motivating Sound, Inc. into a successful nationwide corporation had not been an idle pipe dream. With the help of competent people, success was now within reach. Except, that is, for adequate capitalization. We did not have that. But there was something else. Something so important, that a virtual tornado of conflicting thoughts tumbled through my consciousness. I needed time to think.

Here I was, having spent nearly two weeks away from my family, chasing the dream of unlimited opportunities. What was I sacrificing? What was I gaining? What would I be losing?

Or could I have both? Here I was subjecting myself to enormous stress. I needed to talk to my Heavenly Father, which I did frequently. This night, especially, I needed to calm the turmoil of my mind. With that I went to bed.

My working days often exceeded sixteen hours, especially during the time of the relentless stress brought on by searching for ways to survive. I had worked hard to build the businesses. Now Motivating Sound Inc. threatened to become lost in imminent bankruptcy. My family and employees relied on me to find a way for the business and paychecks to continue. To make matters worse, I was informed that our best dealership in Canada had declared bankruptcy and, worse yet, had not paid the several thousand dollars it owed us. We didn't have the capitalization to survive such a devastating blow.

It was also when an eye specialist, treating the loss of vision in one of my eyes, explained that it was his preliminary diagnosis that I had multiple sclerosis (MS). Before then I knew nothing about MS. But what I heard from others didn't sound good. As my vision gradually started returning, I decided to ignore it. What I could not ignore was that, barring a miracle, our company would have to declare bankruptcy. But, by literally working day and night searching for a way to avoid bankruptcy, I succeeded in selling most of our

> "WHEN IT GETS DARKEST, THE STARS COME OUT."
>
> AUTHOR UNKNOWN

inventory to our Vancouver B.C. distributor. That gave us just enough money to pay our debts, return all the money to my friends who had invested in the company and also a very small gain.

Losing other people's money had always been my greatest fear. Fortunately, I was able to avoid that. The good Lord had answered my frequent prayers and I was grateful. We dissolved Motivating Sound Incorporated. Failure is always painful but it need not be fatal unless we refuse to learn from it and use the bitter lessons with a determination not to repeat the same mistakes in future endeavors.

Major changes

I don't think anyone ever starts a business with the expectation that it's going to fail. But it happens. It happened to me and I can never change that. But I determined that I wouldn't allow it to destroy me.

I had long known that we were seriously undercapitalized for our ambitious undertakings. However, I was relieved because we were able to pay all our corporate debts including our investors. Besides, I still had the retail store and the radio station as well as the Lynden Travel Agency which we had started in our efforts to get our business closer to the break-even point. The travel agency was operated by my associate and good friend, Rook VanHalm. We remained good friends and still get together for lunch regularly to this day.

I began dreaming and planning all the things I could do to expand both the retail as well as our broadcasting business. I could not have known the life-threatening problems that were yet to come.

Full speed ahead

The Musical Instrument Show and Convention brought me to the huge Moscone Convention Center in San Francisco. I had invited two music teachers from Lynden school to attend with me. It was part of my plan to broaden and expand our retail business by adding musical instruments. Though I knew nothing about them, early in life I became acquainted with band music through my late father who, in 1922, had been the founder and first director of the Dutch Bicycle Show Band Crescendo which later became world famous.

"A LIFE WITHOUT OBSTACLES, RISKS AND PROBLEMS WOULD BE BORING"

SID BARON

At the convention we spent a busy afternoon looking at the various factory displays filled with every musical instrument imaginable. Neither myself nor music teachers Gary and Holly had ever seen so many beautiful and shiny instruments in one place. I respected those two teachers who, in a short time, had excelled in turning the Lynden Public High School music department into one of the best in the county. As we sat enjoying a drink and a good discussion in the restaurant of the Marriott Hotel after a delicious dinner, I said: "Gary, you are a semi-professional trumpet player who often plays at weddings and parties. What is your favorite brand?" Without hesitation he said, "Yamaha is, in my opinion, the very best." He went on to say his personal trumpet was a Yamaha and that he'd like his students to get Yamaha instruments. However, the Bellingham band instrument dealer didn't sell them. After thinking for a few seconds I asked Gary if I could negotiate with Yamaha to have them appoint me as a dealer. Gary said he would recommend Yamaha instruments to all his beginner students as well as their parents. The following day I signed on as the exclusive Yamaha musical instrument dealer for Whatcom County.

As I continued to wander through the various exhibits, I was attracted by the sound of beautiful organ music. I walked to where the music originated and was met by an impressive display of Thomas Electronic Organs. The person demonstrating was none other than Bob Ralston from the *Lawrence Welk Show* which was popular on TV at the time. Ralston was an attractive young man who seemingly switched from rousing polka music to waltz and then classical Bach without any effort. My heart skipped a beat as I thought about the possibility of adding electronic organs to my store inventory.

Before long, after negotiating credit arrangements with the suppliers, our electronic retail store was full of merchandise including musical instruments, electronic organs and pianos.

I did not lack confidence in my ability to sell and make my customers happy. Instead, my major worry was that I knew nothing about music. Though my dad had been an accomplished musician, band and choir director, I never showed an interest in learning music. To sell electronic organs effectively I needed to be able to demonstrate how easy it was to learn to play. Over time, during the few spare minutes I could find in the day or evening, I learned how to demonstrate Thomas organs to beginners. For those who were already accomplished on the keyboard I asked Jerry, who was general manager of our radio station, to do the demonstrations. Jerry was quite accomplished on the organ and played in churches and was in demand as an organ soloist. Having a well-stocked store allowed me to concentrate on serving an increasing number of customers with a good variety of merchandise.

Working six days a week, plus being responsible for the radio station on Sundays, made me very busy. It was enjoyable and, best of all, I no longer needed to worry about being unprofitable and near bankruptcy. Negotiating the Thomas organ dealer franchise had been a good move. As big ticket items they also had excellent profit margins. The Thomas factory representative called on us regularly and we brainstormed many promotional ideas. Though we were located in the small town of Lynden, I learned that we did better than many big town dealers. One day the rep suggested that I might consider having Bob Ralston come to Lynden and entertain an audience while demonstrating Thomas organs. During the 1970s the *Lawrence Welk Show* was very popular and Bob Ralston was one of its well known stars. It was costly to have a man with the stature of Bob Ralston come to town. But the idea was exciting and I couldn't let it go. I looked into the availability of a large facility with a stage that could accommodate at least a half dozen organs and seating for close to a thousand people. With the help of Mr. Jones, the factory representative, we managed to make arrangements for the concert.

I was ecstatic that we had booked someone famous to come to Lyndon and, even though the date was about four months into the future, right away began planning promotions for the huge event. Within days I had 2500 five-dollar admission tickets printed. Until they ran out, every customer who came into the store was given an admission ticket stamped with FREE in large letters. Even if a customer didn't make a purchase they were happy because they received something for free.

To promote the concert I used direct mail, purchased radio spots and ran newspaper ads until my supply of tickets was almost gone. I was betting that many ticket holders would not come since there wouldn't be enough standing room.

On the day before the concert it was nearly seven o'clock p.m. when I literally dragged my weary body three blocks along the sidewalk from 525 Front Street, where our store was located, to our home at 211 Front Street. Margaret and the children had been eagerly awaiting my arrival. They were hungry and Margaret had tried her best to keep the food warm. She then looked at me as I sagged into my chair at the head of the table. With a somewhat alarmed expression on her face she said: "Hon, what's the matter? You look sick." I looked at my dear wife and said: "I'm more than just tired but I don't think I'm sick." With that the children seemed relieved. I explained that maybe a little food would make me feel better. However the next morning, when I awoke, my body was numb from head to toe, my hands felt cold and my feet were hot. Somehow I managed to get dressed. Margaret tried to talk me out of going to work. I told her I normally wouldn't go in when I wasn't feeling well, but this was such a big day. Bob Ralston and his wife were coming and I had to introduce him to the audience that evening. We were also going out for dinner with them after the concert. I told her it was something I couldn't get out of doing. Though she understood, my condition still had her worried. Then she stood up and said, "You are my life." Hearing that I stood, hugged her and, with an emotion-laden voice said, "You are *my* life." An hour later she dropped me off at the store. That day, my loyal employees brought much of our store's organ inventory to the concert hall. There they displayed the various models of organs on the stage along with colorful signs.

Bob Ralston and his wife arrived shortly before the start of the program. He introduced us to his wife, who was dressed in an authentic Friesian costume—which was very beautiful. I recognized her dress because the Dutch province of Friesland was where I was born. I had no idea that Bob Ralston's wife was born in the same small province, which was known for speaking its own Friesian language rather than just a dialect. It was fun speaking with her in my native language. In the excitement I forced myself to forget about my weariness and numbness. The place was packed and Bob put on a wonderful concert after which he received a rousing standing ovation.

The following day our store was crowded with customers. It was Saturday and I was working alone from opening until closing. The only thing I could feel good about was that I sold several Thomas organs that day. When it was finally time to close I locked the front door and began to shuffle toward home.

As I walked in the direction of our home a car pulled up behind me. The window rolled down and I heard a familiar voice. It was my dear wife Margaret who said in broken English: "Will you ride wit me in my karr?" It brought a smile to my face together with pleasant memories of long ago. The children loved to tease me about my unconventional Dutch immigrant way of asking a girl for a date. That was exactly what I had asked her one Sunday evening many years before after a church service. We could not have known then that it would be the beginning of a lifelong relationship. Margaret parked the car in front of the house and we covered the short distance up the sidewalk in silence. After dinner as we sat in our living room Margaret said: "Sid I know you've been feeling awful lately, especially the last two very busy days. But I know you and you haven't been feeling well for some time. I can tell even though you don't complain." "You're right hon," I said. "I think I know what it is." Margaret was looking at me with a worried expression on her face waiting for me to explain. "Six years ago when I lost vision in one eye the doctor told me that the problem was in my optic nerve which could be a first indication of Multiple Sclerosis." I went on to explain that while my vision came back it most likely was a warning sign. But rather than slow down I worked harder and put in more hours than ever.

I was truly burning the candle on both ends. I knew that I had MS and was worried. As things deteriorated, I made some telephone inquiries to people I knew were dealing with MS and learned about a specialist at the University of Oregon Medical Center named Doctor Roy Swank. Dr. Swank had recently retired from being the head of the Medical Center's Neurology department where he had devoted most of his life as a research scientist specializing in Multiple Sclerosis. The next Monday, Margaret and I walked into the office of Dr. Swank. He offered us a chair and with a warm smile gave us a welcoming but firm handshake. He was of average height and build with fine facial features and twinkling eyes. "Okay Sid," he began, "tell me why you think you have MS." I told him about the loss of vision some years ago and the numerous tests which had all been inconclusive. Then I told him about my first hospitalization with an infection of unknown origin and subsequent hospitalizations because of serious urinary tract infections. He nodded his head with understanding when I told him about my extreme weariness and extensive numbness throughout my body. Then he listened intently before explaining, "Sid there is no test that will, beyond the shadow of a doubt, confirm that a patient has MS. There is always the possibility that a patient's symptoms closely mimic MS. But based on the symptoms you've described, I know that you have MS and that I need not subject you to additional tests."

Dr. Swank proceeded to tell us that many of his years of research had been devoted to helping MS patients survive this mysterious and incurable disease. There was no ambiguity in his words when he explained that I needed to reduce the stress in my life and that both Margaret and I needed to assume responsibility for my survival. He said, "Sid, if you follow the recommendations I provide you with, you will feel better five years from now than you feel right now." I said "Okay, Dr. Swank. But I would rather have you wave a magic wand or give me a magic potion if that would cure me more quickly. Five years is a long time." I assured him we would do whatever we needed to if it meant surviving the disease with minimum incapacitating damage. Dr. Swank smiled approvingly and said that there were two characteristics that were very important in managing MS. Through listening to and observing me, he felt I had both those characteristics. Naturally I was curious and asked what those characteristics were. He answered, "An optimistic spirit, and an easy laugh with a good sense of humor."

I liked Dr. Swank and, as we left, asked if he minded if I told a joke. After assuring me it was okay, I told him the following:

To celebrate the end of World War ll, Prime Minister Churchill was invited to attend a warm and dignified reception with the Queen. They were driven in a classic 1934 Bentley to the edge of central London, where they changed to a magnificent 17th century carriage hitched to six white horses. They continue on toward Buckingham Palace, waving to the thousands of cheering Brits. All was going well until suddenly the right rear horse lets fly the most horrendous earth shattering fart ever heard in the British Empire. The smell was atrocious and both passengers in the carriage used handkerchiefs over their noses. The fart practically shook the coach, but the two dignitaries of State did their best to ignore the incident. The Queen then turned to Churchill and said, "Mr. Prime Minister, please accept my regrets. I am sure you understand there are some things that even a Queen cannot control." Churchill, trying to be proper replied, "Your Majesty, do not give the matter another thought... until you mentioned it, I thought it was one of the horses."

"THERE IS NO DOUBT IN MY MIND THAT MY LIGHTHEARTED SENSE OF HUMOR WAS AND IS A VERY IMPORTANT INGREDIENT IN SURVIVING MULTIPLE SCLEROSIS."

SID BARON

From "How I survived Multiple Sclerosis and Thrived for more than 40 years"

Dr. Swank was holding his stomach and he couldn't quit laughing. "Okay Sid," he said, "I want to see you once a year and I'll never let you leave without telling me another joke."

Margaret and I stayed overnight in a Portland hotel. Before leaving for Lynden the next morning I went to a bookstore and bought a book on how to become a good delegator. I knew that my stress-filled business life would have to change if I didn't want to become totally disabled. Diet-wise, Margaret knew that her choice of ingredients and food preparation would also change drastically.

From Portland heading north on I-5, Lynden is about 300 miles away. Margaret was reading the MS book written by Dr. Swank and Barbara Dugan, his nutritionist. We were mostly silent because I was lost in contemplation. I needed to accept the fact that I had an incurable disease and that there was a possibility that no matter how I changed my life, my eating habits and my work, there were no guarantees. There was a likelihood I could soon become totally disabled and bound to a wheelchair.

Suddenly I realized that my consciousness had filled me with a storm of negative thoughts. I am a firm believer that there is nothing positive about negative thinking. For many years I had been blessed with boundless energy. The thought that I would someday lose my health and energy had never entered my mind during all of my working years. Yes, I realized that we usually take the blessings of our lives for granted. Then, completely unexpected, life throws everyone a curve-ball. It might not be what we wanted but we have to deal with new realities. To do that we have choices to make. We can either decide that the damage of being hit by that curve ball will be completely devastating or we can dig deeper into our inner self and decide that we will do everything we can to survive. I still had a burning desire to make my ventures successful. Would I still be able to accomplish that with fading energies and the knowledge that I had an incurable disease? Yes, by the grace of God, I could!

If you focus on the negative you end up burying your dreams and passions of life. In doing so you would be burying a big part of yourself and who you are. That would be a form of dying.

I walked into my store wearing gloves. Not because the weather was cold but because my hands were plagued with a combination of numbness, a tingling sensation and feeling cold. I knew the cause for my relentless stress was selling merchandise to customers all day long, oftentimes without breaking for lunch. Now I was in the process of reducing my stress. This required me to appoint Mary VanderPol, who was a pleasant, outgoing and engaging person, as the primary salesperson in the store (to this day we still are friends with Mary and her husband Marv). One day Mary came into my office and hurriedly said, "Sid, someone is looking at an organ." Electronic organs were big ticket items and we had agreed that I would wait on any prospective organ customers. I quickly got up from my desk and removed my gloves before greeting the prospective buyer. She was an attractive lady, probably in her mid-thirties, with beautiful black curly hair combined with slightly olive skin and stunning greenish-blue eyes. I noticed what appeared to be a very expensive diamond wedding ring. Mentally combining that knowledge with what appeared to be expensive clothing, I steered her in the direction of a fairly high-end Thomas organ.

She explained that her only experience with a keyboard was some years ago while in high school when she took a few piano lessons. The Thomas organ had caught her attention due to its exclusive "Color-Glo" feature which made it very easy to learn. Her goal was to get her children to learn how to play but now that they were teenagers and busy with friends, she exclaimed that it was probably too late to get them started. I nodded with complete agreement. Sitting on the organ bench I said, "Mrs. Davis this is one of the most popular models. I wish I could give you an impressive demonstration but you're ahead of me because you learned to read music and I can't read a note." Flipping the switch to the "on" position, all the while maintaining eye contact, I said, "I'll demonstrate how easy it is to play this amazing Thomas organ." The music book showed the notes in various colors that matched the colors that were lighting up inside the keys. I paged through the music book and found "When the Saints Go Marching In." I didn't tell her that it was the only selection I had learned to play. She was fascinated with the demonstration. "Okay, Mrs. Davis. I'm going to play it again, but this time I'm going to play it quite different. I'll change the flute sounds to saxophone and trumpet sounds." While explaining I pushed various keys, known on an organ as "stops." I also played it a little louder by pressing heavier on the pedal. Mrs. Davis commented that it was like pushing on the gas pedal of a car. It was a good analogy. I then added drums and other percussion sounds. I joked that if she felt like marching along, that was okay. Being in the mood for showing off, and having noticed her low cut dress showing off her cleavage, I knew she couldn't be shy. At this point I played, "When the Saints Go Marching In" with all the flair, power and percussion at my command. I could tell my prospect was impressed since she tapped her toes with the rhythm of the marching band music.

By the time I finished she couldn't refrain from clapping her hands and saying: "Mr. Baron, it's hard to believe you didn't have any music education. How long did it take you to learn to play like that?" I looked straight into her eyes and said, "Honestly, Mrs. Davis, it took me one afternoon to learn. This is an instrument every member of your family can play in a very short time." She remarked how impressed she was, but that she didn't dare ask how much it cost. I soon realized that the trickiest part of closing a sale had arrived—the part that made my heart beat faster. Especially as I mentally calculated the profit margin on the sale of a $2600 electronic organ. It was the 1970s and $2600 was a heap of money. I explained that when one calculated the fun each member of the family could have by playing this organ, then the 36 monthly payments would really seem like a bargain. (This was during a simpler time, before the advent of TV games, cell phones and texting.) I could tell my prospect was thoroughly sold and invited her into our closing office. She offered a down payment of $1000 and said she'd be able to pay the balance in twenty-four months.

At that time the bank would immediately pay us the full amount of the contract and then collect the payments as well as 9.5 percent interest on the balance. A few months earlier I decided that because our business was doing well, I would be able to handle our own financing in the form of an in-house conditional sales contract which allowed the customer to make payments directly to the store. When the customer made a purchase I would pay the store the full amount of the sale. I would then receive the monthly payments plus the interest. Margaret was in charge of preparing and mailing the monthly statements. That marked our entry into the financing business.

Back then I could never imagined that, at the time of this writing, Baron Credit Corporation would still be in business.

My wonderful employees all helped in reducing my stress level. Rook, my friend and partner, operated the Lynden Travel Agency. Jerry managed KLYN-FM, which was increasingly gaining listeners as well as advertisers. The retail store performed well but, as we approached the 1980s and the increasing appearance of large chain stores, the writing was on the wall as the retail world became more competitive. In addition changes in technology were multiplying. We made the transition from vacuum tubes in radios, TVs, amplifiers and other electronic equipment to solid state components. But our service department was seriously affected by the changing technology.

In the early 1980s the Federal Communications Commission required the break-up of AT&T. This resulted in allowing competition in the telephone business for the first time. In response, we decided to phase out our electronic repair shop and get involved in the sales and service of commercial telecommunication systems. To house our major business activities, I succeeded in purchasing the building we had rented for many years. A year later I purchased the adjoining building. This was ideal for relocating the growing travel agency. The upper floor of that building included four apartment units which made it possible to supply some of our broadcast station personnel with very affordable housing. This was my first entry in owning commercial real estate.

I had no plans for getting into any other real estate ownership beyond what was required to house my current businesses. Clearly, I didn't have a crystal ball. However, what I did have was an incurable disease. Even though my multiple sclerosis was largely in remission, occasional attacks of serious fatigue reminded me that I would never again have the energy I had taken for granted for so long. While I was adhering closely to Dr. Swank's advice, I had done enough research to know that the possibility of becoming disabled could never be ruled out.

Though we had done well the past few years, I knew there were changes on the horizon and that business would become more challenging. If my health permitted, I knew I would continue to do well. But I also needed to analyze the future just in case I was not able to continue working. While remaining a positive optimist, at the same time I needed to be pragmatic. Envisioning a worst-case scenario, I knew my family was far from being on "easy street." Of my various businesses, the most personally fulfilling was the radio station. It gave me an opportunity to employ young high school seniors and, in many cases, serve as a mentor—which is something I firmly believed in. It was something I could do for others that was more important than what I could do for myself.

The radio station also gave me a "voice" in the community. We always broadcast the Lynden Public and Christian high school games. I also enjoyed preparing my daily three-to-four minute segment called "Another Point of View." The weekly interview program featured various people from the community and was always stimulating. We not only covered politics but also topics that dealt with why marriages fail, death, parental wisdom, the importance of faith and other important issues. The program allowed listeners the opportunity to call in their viewpoints. I believe the radio station provided me a platform for applying creative new ideas. From the first day KLYN-FM became operational I knew I would never have to retire because owning the station would always allow me to choose broadcasting activities that would keep my brain in gear and avoid cognitive decline.

"I BELIEVE ONE OF THE MOST CRUCIAL QUALITIES FOR ENTREPRENEURS TO SUCCEED IS SELF-MOTIVATION. WITHOUT BEING SELF-MOTIVATED YOU WILL ALWAYS FIND YOURSELF PUTTING THINGS OFF AND AS A ENTREPRENEUR, YOU WILL NOT SUCCEED."

SID BARON

Those thoughts never took into account that I might have to deal with an incurable disease that often rendered patients unable to continue working resulting in the possibility of living in poverty. Now, in my late forties, I needed to add a worst-case scenario to my contemplations. Prayer was always a regular part of our family life. But I was still responsible for doing all that was possible to maintain my health and the economic well-being of my family. No matter what the future held, I knew my faith would never fade. By this time our older children were getting married and our family financial obligations were declining. Neither Margaret nor I ever had a need to live "high on the hog." We were happy living modestly. Though I was still relatively young, if I weren't able to work anymore we'd soon be poor. A net worth of around two-hundred thousand dollars would soon dissipate especially with the rampant inflation the country was experiencing at the time. It was at that point when I first began to wonder what the value of my radio station might be. I pleasantly discovered that the value of the radio station was such that if I sold it I could be a millionaire.

I had always assumed complete responsibility for taking care of my wife and family. By selling KLYN-FM, I would no longer need to worry about our family finances. The decision was not easy. For many years I have often wished I still owned the radio station. A few years later I sold the electronic telecommunications business to my oldest son Jim and employee Phil Bratt who still successfully operates Baron Telecommunications. After a close-out sale, the retail store was history. My good friend and partner Rook Van Halm continued to manage the Lynden Travel agency for many years until it too was closed.

I call this section of the chapter "toward the end of an era." Now I was retired and could finally take life easy. I also wouldn't need to worry any more about being incapacitated by MS. Yes, my physical energies were not what they used to be but my mental energies were unaffected. I could never succeed in putting my brain in neutral. That's the reason I want to tell you about…

The changes in my business life didn't happen overnight. Margaret and I discussed every idea I proposed. We were doing all we could to help me survive MS but we both knew there would be no guarantees. Because we understood what poverty was, we weren't anxious to live our remaining life in that condition. Selling the radio station provided for our financial needs and the gradual disposition of the other business activities allowed me to live a "stress-free" life.

Humor is very important in reducing stress and improving health. But as long as we still have entrepreneurial or ambitious dreams there is still stress in our lives. Dreaming, thinking or planning what you might still be able to accomplish is positive stress. Worrying about all the things that could go wrong is negative stress.

CHAPTER EIGHT

SURROUND YOURSELF WITH TALENT:

HIRE THE BEST AND THEY'LL DO THE REST

I worked with Sid in the hotel business from 1995-2010, until he sold his last hotel. Now I work for the company that purchased one of his hotels and am overseeing several other properties. My time with Sid was generally spent in meetings, oftentimes over lunch. He was already in his sixties when I started working with him, a time when others his age are thinking of retirement. But not Sid, I think he sees going to work as relaxation and stress relief. Our meetings, which stretched over two hours, were more about how to approach our work rather than about details. He also wanted to know how we were doing personally and about our families.

Sid is not a hands-on type of owner. His biggest asset is spotting talent. He's very good at finding the people who know how to do what he's not experienced in doing himself. For example at Exxel Pacific he partnered with Kevin DeVries, who's an amazing talent. Sid saw certain abilities in him and that choice led to the success they've had.

In my business relationship with Sid he gave me a lot of freedom to make decisions at the property level and to make mistakes so that I could learn from them. He was always there to help if I needed it. Sid pushed me (even if at times it was uncomfortable) to follow up on my decisions. If I made the wrong decisions I also had to fix them on my own. In doing so he allowed me to learn about the business through the school of hard knocks. Many owners like to micro-manage, which can be very tough on a manager and limits their ability to learn. Sid empowered me to make decisions which, for my career, were very beneficial.

Sid has always been willing to invest in his employees, including myself, through educational opportunities. Any time there was a conference or seminar that could further my education or make me a more valuable asset to the company, he invested in my participation. He took to heart the philosophy of hiring and promoting from within by selecting line staff to become managers.

When there were disputes with customers I always knew that Sid had my back. He understood that fine line between doing one's best to please people without giving away the farm. On those rare occasions when a guest wanted to speak directly with Sid or someone else at the corporate office, he backed me up. He might have disagreed with my decision, but he supported it with the customer and then would later discuss it with me to determine how I might handle it better the next time.

Sid understands his own limitations and never allows his ego to get in the way. Instead he goes out and finds people who compliment his weaknesses and strengths. Even though Sid never actually managed a hotel, he understood the operations enough to know what type of people he needed. He is very good at doing his research and knows what he's getting into in terms of risks and rewards. Sid also knows the importance of not taking things too seriously. He believes if one cannot laugh at themselves (or laugh at work) they will not enjoy their job and are instead just putting in time. Not only did he want his employees to enjoy their work, he also wanted them to enjoy their time away from work. He was always encouraging his employees to take vacations. While it was costly in the short run, it made for better and happier employees whose work, in the long run, paid off.

For me, working with Sid was a pleasure I'll never forget. He has been a great influence on me.

—Loren Terpstra, is a Certified Hotel Administrator with a degree in hospitality management. He currently serves as the operations manager for the various hotels owned by Hollander Investments Inc. He lives in Lynden, Washington with his wife and children.

Moving Forward

After closing the store there were no more customer purchases to finance. Yet with over a hundred thousand in receivables, monthly statements needed to go out. Because computers, scanners, copiers and other time-saving office equipment had arrived on the scene, I decided to expand my little financing business to include leasing. I contacted a computer dealer in the area as well as some office equipment retailers and offered my leasing services. Rarely did I see the equipment being leased. It was mostly a matter of approving the dealer's prospective customer with the collateral being the equipment identified on the lease contract. I incorporated that business under the name Baron Credit Corporation. When the company who supplied the equipment submitted all the lease forms, properly signed with the first and last lease payment checks attached, the vendor

"BOYS, THERE AIN'T NO FREE LUNCHES IN THIS COUNTRY. AND DON'T GO SPENDING YOUR WHOLE LIFE COMMISERATING THAT YOU GOT THE RAW DEALS. YOU'VE GOT TO SAY, I THINK THAT IF I KEEP WORKING AT THIS AND WANT IT BAD ENOUGH I CAN HAVE IT. IT'S CALLED PERSEVERANCE."

LEE IACOCCA

was paid the full selling price. The leasing company, Baron Credit Corporation, received the monthly lease payments, including interest over the next thirty-six to sixty months.

In 1982 I decided to aggressively expand the leasing activities. It was triggered by an awareness of the economics of inflation which, at the time, seemed unstoppable by the Federal Reserve Board. I knew that run-away inflation can only be tamed by increasing interest rates. Prior to that, the administration of President Carter seemed reluctant to slow down the overheated economy. But that began to change when President Ronald Reagan was inaugurated in 1981. During that time, the Federal Reserve increased the prime rate until, in early 1982, it reached a staggering 22 percent! These days an interest rate that high seems unbelievable with current interest rates the lowest in recent history.

Back then it wasn't possible to get a bank loan at prime. Computers had arrived on the scene and the dealers selling them found few customers with the cash to buy a computer system outright. At that time a computer system, including a printer, was priced in excess of $10,000. Here's where my planning and calculations went into high gear. I knew banks couldn't afford to loan money at the prime rate since banks would typically add two to three percentage points to prime. I knew if my lease rates were based on 23 percent it would be lower than the average small business was able to negotiate with their bank. A great opportunity was knocking and I responded. All leases in excess of $7500 were written for a sixty-month term. I knew that as soon as inflation began to decline, the Feds would begin reducing interest rates. The sixty-month lease term never included a variable interest factor. Therefore the lease contracts I wrote at the 23 percent would remain at that rate for the entire five-year term. While the money I needed to borrow from my friendly banker was also costly due to the high interest rates I was paying, my rate was subject to being adjusted monthly. Luckily my "crystal ball" served me well and it wasn't long before interest rates came down. Needless to say, for a few years Baron Credit Corporation was very profitable.

***

Beyond raising our six children, Margaret also had her own "long-term dreams." She was frugal and for many years knew that we didn't have money for any luxuries. For the longest time she dreamed about building a new house. She was always good at interior design and loved the idea of being completely in charge of decorating a new home. By this time we no longer had financial worries so we decided to purchase a lot. Before construction began we were approached by our friend Mike who we had known a few years. Mike explained that he had built a brand new home right next to his own impressive estate complete with swimming pool and tennis court. We decided to inspect it. His new home was a beautiful two story with underground car parking. Mike had studied architectural design and was very good at designing homes with a distinctive New England flair. We decided to purchase the house from

Mike and, while not immediately, Margaret eventually did add her own design touches when we later added on. We were neighbors and close friends with Mike, his wife and their children. Our friendship continues to this day.

Mike had told me about an apartment complex he had designed and built in Bellingham which he owned together with a partner. I visited Mike in his office at the apartment complex and he showed me the architectural plans and said he had acted as the general contractor for the project. At the time he was working on the design for another apartment complex to be located not far from the campus of Western Washington State University. He asked if I was interested in joining him as a partner in that project. I was flattered he asked me but explained that I had no idea how something that large, probably costing over two million dollars, could possibly be financed. My previous banking experience was with small loans for short time periods. This was an entirely different endeavor that would require huge loans and extended repayment terms. Mike explained that after a construction site was secured, the architectural plans were finished, pro-forma estimations of rental rates performed and expected occupancy levels met, we would be ready for a professional appraiser.

The professionally licensed MAI (Member of the Appraisal Institute) appraiser would study every aspect of the proposed project and develop a realistic value estimate which the bank would use to determine the amount it could loan. This was in the very early 1980s and nowadays both the economic climate and bank lending criteria are vastly different.

The appraisal for our proposed apartment complex indicated that the value of the completed project was well above our estimated construction costs. This made it possible for us to get 100 percent financing on the entire project. This is referred to as high leverage financing. I would have been comfortable with a more conservative approach because this was new for me—leaving much for me to learn. Approximately one year later I was very pleased to have a 50 percent stake in the ownership of the impressive eighty-unit Cambridge Square apartment complex. It didn't take long before the occupancy was sufficient to make the monthly mortgage payments and only a few months longer before we were able to earn some monthly income from our investment in the partnership.

As the project progressed, Mike and I would meet for lunch at least once a week. After the apartment project was operating smoothly and profitably, it wasn't long before we began talking about other opportunities. Soon we became aware of a small motel located near the freeway in Mount Vernon, Washington being for sale. We traveled the forty miles to the location of the twenty-six unit Norwester Motel to meet with the listing realtor agent. We were not impressed with the property. The exterior as well as the rooms and furniture appeared to have been neglected for years. We discussed the pros and cons of a possible acquisition. The seller was very motivated to dispose of the property which included significant additional land that could be sold or developed. The property was located near the freeway between Vancouver, BC and Portland, OR. If we could sell a couple of sites for a restaurant or other use we could possibly get the funds for a complete remodel of the run-down motel. We made an offer below the asking price and soon were the proud owners of a "junky" motel.

My partner Mike was very creative both as a gifted designer and an experienced builder. While I was creative in many other areas of business, I knew nothing about design or construction. Soon the remodeling was underway. It posed some challenges. We needed to keep as many units intact as possible to accommodate guests since the income from occupied rooms was needed to pay the manager and housekeeping staff while helping to make the mortgage payments. Gradually all twenty-six rooms were refurbished and furniture replaced. Soon the motel qualified as franchised property by a large national chain. The name was changed, the occupancy increased and we were soon ready to add more rooms. Eventually it grew to sixty-six rooms. Many times during the summer months we were booked to capacity.

With a contractor friend, Mike and I established an additional partnership to build and own a small office building on a parcel of land we owned immediately adjacent to the motel. Since there were now three partners involved we called the project the "Tri-Dex Office Building." A year or two later the third partner purchased the building and became its sole owner.

With both the apartment complex in Bellingham and the motel in Mount Vernon operating profitably, Mike and I began to discuss the possibility of building a new hotel in Bellingham. There is always a great deal of due diligence involved before a major decision can be made. That research includes determining the best location for a hotel, the availability of land, the cost of construction, projected income and expense analyses, our borrowing capacity and other feasibility analyses. Once those criteria were met, less than two years later we built a beautiful new eighty-room hotel affiliated with a national franchise. We hired staff including a manager, housekeeping personnel and front desk agents. The hotel was an instant success. We were soon able to pay the salaries and expenses as well as the mortgage payments from its profits.

But Mike was not about to allow us to rest on our accomplishments. It wasn't long before we acquired some additional land near the new hotel. Mike again put on his architectural design hat and prepared plans for a two-floor commercial office building. Around a year later our Meridian Place office and retail building was nearing completion. This was a totally different area of business activity. To make Meridian Place successful we would have to find tenants to occupy space in its nearly 35,000 square feet of retail and office space. We agreed to hire a young man named Kevin DeVries who had just graduated from Dordt College in Iowa.

While in college, Mike's son Mark had become a close friend of Kevin. I got to know Kevin during summer vacations when he visited his friend Mark. Initially he was hired to be our leasing agent for Meridian Place. Once that project was nearly finished, Mike turned his attention toward the next expansion plan which involved an IRS-1031 tax deferred sale of our Cambridge Square apartment complex to acquire a struggling Holiday Inn hotel in Texas. By this time I had become uncomfortable with the speed of our expansion plans and regarded the acquisition of a large hotel in Texas as too risky.

> **"I HAVE FOUND NO GREATER SATISFACTION THAN ACHIEVING SUCCESS THROUGH HONEST DEALING AND STRICT ADHERENCE TO THE VIEW THAT, FOR YOU TO GAIN, THOSE YOU DEAL WITH SHOULD GAIN AS WELL."**
>
> ALAN GREENSPAN

Mike, who is ten years younger and less risk averse, had a different outlook. We decided to divide our assets, dissolve the partnership and go our separate ways. Both being Christian, we accomplished the dissolution in a mutually agreeable, peaceful and friendly manner. As I write this, Mike has succeeded in building a sizable hotel empire and we continue to be good friends. In the process of dividing our properties, I became the owner of the nearly fished Meridian Place commercial building and Kevin was now my employee.

One morning on my way to my office, which was now located in Meridian Place, I was driving along East Bakerview Street when I noticed a sign that read: "This site approved for eighty apartment units." It included the name and telephone number of the real estate listing agent. That triggered an idea. When I arrived at my office I picked up the telephone book and opened it to the "Apartments" section of the yellow pages to do a little independent research. Pretending to be someone interested in renting an apartment, I called several existing apartment complexes. What I learned excited me. There were virtually no vacancies in Bellingham.

Later on over lunch with Kevin that day I announced that I had an idea. Kevin, who is a young man of few words, nodded and listened attentively. Handing him the name and telephone number of the real estate agent, I asked him to do some research on that property—determine price, suitability for construction of an apartment building, county and city permits required and requirements cost, income and expense projection and anything else we'd want to know before purchasing the building site.

> "AS I BEGAN TO READ ABOUT PEOPLE OF ACCOMPLISHMENT, IT DAWNED ON ME THAT THE PERSON WHO HAS THE MOST TO DO WITH WHAT HAPPENS IN YOUR LIFE IS—YOU."
>
> DR. BEN CARSON

One would normally expect someone to be busy writing notes as I barked my commands. With Kevin it did not surprise me that he took no written notes. I had already learned that when Mike and I had our regular meetings with Kevin to suggest possible potential tenants for Meridian Place, he never took notes. To my amazement he never forgot a single detail. He was simply a brilliant young man. Of course I had prepared spreadsheet projections similar to the sample on page 112.

The projections were based on the cost of construction not to exceed two-and-a-half million dollars and that our bank loan was not to exceed two million. When we met with the officials of our construction company we learned that the cost of constructing the complex using the plans as prepared by our architect would approach three million dollars. This led us to secure the services of another architect who prepared plans that would fit our budget. During this process, Kevin took care of nearly every detail. Then during construction we began receiving applications from prospective tenants. We knew the apartment rental market in Bellingham was good. Even so, we had not expected that within approximately two weeks from construction completion, Bakerview Terrace apartments would be fully occupied. It turned out to be a very successful investment.

SAMPLE

1982 Projections

Name: Bakerview Terrace Apartments

Units: 78

Annual Income

Average monthly rent $365.00 per unit and (costs)

Monthly income

Description	Monthly	Annual
90% occupied	$25,550.00	$306,600.00
Monthly mortgage payment	-$15,400.00	-$184,800.00
Manager salary	-$1,000.00	-$12,000.00
Maintenance	-$250.00	-$3,000.00
Common area utilities	$175.00	+$2,100.00
Property taxes	-$4,850.00	-$58,200.00
Misc. expenses	-$1,200.00	-$14,400.00
Net monthly P&(L)	$3,025.00	$36,300.00

"Kevin," I began, "you have done a great job bringing Bakerview Terrace Apartments to fruition. I want you to know that I'm impressed and, as a result, I'm going to give you a small percentage of ownership in the project." With that I handed him an envelope with his ownership percentage certificate though, looking back now, I don't think he thought that his accomplishment was anything special. He was a modest young man and bragging about himself was simply unthinkable. I told him I didn't know what or when there would be a next project or what it might be, but that I thought we should have a lawyer prepare a partnership agreement. From then on whatever and whenever we planned another project, Kevin and I would be equal partners. That was the birth of the "Exxel Development Group" partnership. Using the word "group" seemed to imply that we might consider the possibility of adding additional partners in the future. That might have crossed my mind, but the word "group" always remained a partnership just between Kevin and myself.

Forming a new partnership meant the bookkeeper, who handled the accounting work for Baron Credit Corporation as well as the sixty-six unit motel in Mount Vernon and newly finished Meridian Place, needed to add the Bakerview Terrace apartments accounting to her responsibilities. Since Baron Credit Corporation specialized in financing leased office electronic equipment we operated primarily under the assumed trade name of Business Equipment Leasing (BEL).

It now became my sincere desire to help Exxel Development Group (EDG) and my new partner succeed. Kevin and I had not known each other for a long time but had already discovered we had much in common. I was born and raised on a small farm in Holland. A generation later, Kevin was born and raised on a small farm in the state of Iowa. His parents were very close to the same age as Margaret and me. Both our parents were devout Christians and were members of the same denomination. We both believed that, as Christians, the conduct of our lives would not be measured by our regular church attendance. Instead our lives were about how we affected and related to others whose lives were touched by ours. Whether customers or competitors were rich or poor, important or of lowly status, everyone deserved to be treated with respect and honesty. Those were the core principles which we both believed should never be compromised.

For many weeks we pondered how we could start a new business. We had available retail space in my Meridian Place building, which Kevin managed. Many ideas were explored and rejected. One day we had arranged a lunch meeting with the man who had been the superintendent employed by the contractor during the construction of Bakerview Terrace. He told us how much he enjoyed working with us and suggested we start a construction company. If we did, he said he'd love to work for us. Kevin and I looked at each other, undoubtedly both thinking it was an idea that required further discussion. We both had the time to think about the feasibility of getting into that business. Other than off-and-on monitoring of the various projects being built during my partnership with Mike, as well as the construction of our apartment building, I knew next to nothing about reading blueprints, much less turn the drawings into a finished building. It all looked complicated to me and I respected those who had the skills to turn a set of drawings into a beautiful building.

Skill was only one ingredient in construction. It also required a lot of energy and hard work. I was deficient in both areas. My MS continued to, very gradually, nibble away at my level of physical energy. Advancing years would also gradually become an inescapable factor. But Kevin was my partner now and I needed to think about him. He was a generation younger, full of energy and ambition. He was also a quick learner. His brother in Iowa had a large and growing electrical contracting business. During Kevin's high school as well as college years he worked in his brother's business during summer vacations. The pros and cons of getting into the general contracting business were extensively discussed. We now had a very nice young man with extensive construction experience willing to come and work for us. Unlike other businesses I had started in the past, I knew that starting a general contracting business could not be done on a proverbial "shoestring." There would soon be bills to pay to subcontractors, along with wages and other costs that were part of operating any business. We needed start-up money and knew we didn't have a track record that would satisfy any bank wanting to loan us money. I suggested that with all the resources available to Baron Credit Corporation, I would be able to loan the new construction company some initial startup funds. We contacted a lawyer friend and asked him to prepare the documents and incorporate our new business venture under the name Exxel Development Construction Company.

> **"BUILT INTO EVERY PROJECT ARE OPPORTUNITIES NOT TO SUCCEED."**
>
> SUSAN OLASKY

Kevin and I were each issued 50 percent of the shares. Now the challenge was landing our first job as general contractor.

I owned the sixty-six room motel in Mount Vernon, Washington, and visited with the general manager and other staff people there at least once a week. As Kevin and I were contemplating getting the construction company started, we decided that we might be able to duplicate our success in developing Bakerview Terrace by planning another apartment complex in Mount Vernon. The difference would be that the project would be built by our newly established Exxel Development Construction Company. It was a big project that would cost over three million dollars, which was a lot of money in 1989. Fortunately, during my years in business, I had established an excellent credit record with banks. This is an essential ingredient for success. To raise sufficient funds for a down payment or equity on a bank loan we accepted over $500,000 from friends and acquaintances who were eager to share in our new venture. Those were people who had known me for many years and trusted me with their money. That would not have been possible had my reputation been tarnished during my business career.

We were able to complete the Burlington Terrace apartments and operate them successfully. Then, just a few short years later, we sold them and our investor friends were all repaid their original investment along with a respectable percentage of the gains.

The small, run-down motel my previous partner Mike and I had purchased and expanded into a sixty-six room facility, was exceptionally profitable. That led Margaret and I to begin talking about building a nice hotel in Bellingham. Margaret, who has a keen eye for design and interior decorations, was able to participate fully. We purchased the land and spent many months planning and worrying about how to come up with adequate funds for a sizable down payment to Exxel Construction so that work could begin.

I decided to sell our Mount Vernon motel and with the proceeds we had enough money to move ahead with our dream hotel in Bellingham. Exxel Construction built the beautiful eighty-six room Baron Suites hotel. Together with the manager we hired a staff of approximately thirty employees. They included housekeepers, laundry, front desk agents, a night auditor and maintenance person. (In the question and answer chapter I will address my experience with conflict resolution between the housekeeping and front desk staff.) We operated the Baron Suites hotel for many years before selling it in 2011.

Our Exxel Development Construction operation was growing. We built an apartment complex in Bellingham for a client who lived in the Boston area as well as a water view condominium project for clients who resided in the midwest. The construction company was an entity separate from Exxel Development Group (EDG) which was my partnership with Kevin. Initially Kevin and I were the sole owners of the construction company, which we later renamed as Exxel Pacific Construction Inc. (EPC).

EPC was a general contractor firm that specialized in build-only projects for clients. I was the client when they built the

Baron Suites hotel. Kevin and I (EDG) were the clients when Exxel Pacific built the Burlington Terrace Apartments. After that apartment complex was sold I suggested to Kevin that we do some research in an attempt to find a promising location for a small hotel in an area other than Bellingham. We looked at markets in Snohomish County north of Seattle which was home to the huge Boeing Aircraft factory in Everett, WA.

The small town of Monroe is located in the foothills of the Cascade Mountain range approximately thirty miles east of Everett. The Monroe Fairgrounds had numerous events throughout the year and only one small motel which was very old and poorly maintained. We succeeded in purchasing a building site near US-2 which is a main highway connecting the western part of the state, through the Cascade mountains, with the eastern part. My experience in the lodging business had been very positive as well as profitable. We believed that a modest hotel in Monroe would be a good investment. At that time the interest rates on commercial bank loans were running at around 8 percent. If we structured it properly, we would be able to sell small ownership portions to a number of investors. If we borrowed the money from a bank we would have to make monthly payments on the principle and pay the interest. We thought, why not make those payments to our friends and investors?

At that time the relatively simple business structure known as Limited Liability Company (LLC) had not yet been developed. As a result, we had no choice other than to spend significant legal fees in forming a Limited Partnership. Being completely legal in every aspect of our business operations was of paramount importance especially when investor money was involved. Playing questionable "games" in any of our business dealings would never be in harmony with our core values.

The Baron Inn hotel was developed, constructed and furnished without any bank financing. We had more than thirty investors who all received returns on their investments in excess of their expectations. EDG was the general partner and we had an annual dinner meeting with all our limited partners. At the dinner we gave them the year-end dividend check as well as financial and operational information. It also gave them an opportunity to ask us any questions.

The time required to drive from Bellingham to Monroe took about ninety minutes by car. Quite often Kevin and I would take my Cessna Skylane airplane instead of driving and land at the airport not far from the hotel. Someone would then pick us up so we could check on the progress of construction. Often we were there weekly during the building and start-up phase. Operating a hotel is different from managing any other business and often presents unique challenges. One major difference is that hotels are open twenty-four hours, seven days a week, fifty-two weeks a year. I hired the first manager for the Monroe property from a competing hotel located adjacent to the Baron Suites hotel. It was still several weeks before our Monroe property would be completed, giving her ample time to give notice to her current employer. Marcy had several years of hotel management experience. Staff also had to be hired prior to the opening of the hotel. Though the building was not yet fully completed, we were able to conduct job interviews with prospective employees in the hotel meeting room. I was present when Marcy conducted the interviews and watched each prospective employee closely, occasionally asking a question.

Every hotel has a minimum of two separate departments: front desk and housekeeping. For the owner or manager, both departments are equally important but the skills and personalities in selecting employees for each varies significantly.

The "nerve center" of a hospitality operation is the front desk. When a guest enters the lobby that's where they get their first impression. If they are greeted by the front desk agent with a cheery "welcome" and a warm smile, the all-important first impression will be positive. Easy smiles as well as a friendly, polite disposition are essential ingredients required of a successful front desk employee. A number of special skills are also required. Front desk staff must be able to handle reservations, credit card transactions, telephone operations, maintain and update accurate available room statistics and deal diplomatically with any guest complaints.

Lucy had been hired as head of the housekeeping department, and she and I had developed a relationship of mutual trust. She knew what we expected regarding the operation of the Baron Inn hotel. I also knew she would confide in me if, and whenever, she observed activities that were not in our best interest as owners nor in the best interest of guests. I visited the hotel weekly. Approximately one year after opening the hotel Lucy whispered to me, "Sid I'd like to talk to you privately." We discreetly walked along the hallway to the exit door at the rear of the hotel. When we were outside behind the hotel, and even though there was no one in sight, Lucy talked very softly. "Sid" she began, "I don't want to be known as a spy. Please don't let anyone know where you got the information I'm sharing." I assured Lucy that I'd keep everything strictly confidential. Then she looked around, making sure no one saw us. Satisfied that "the coast was clear" she began. "Sid, about six weeks ago Marcy hired her daughter from Las Vegas. Sometimes she helps with housekeeping and sometimes she works at the front desk. I've seen both Marcy and her daughter smoking marijuana." Glancing around suspiciously she continued in a whisper: "You know, I'm the head housekeeper and get here first in the morning when only the night guy is at the front desk. He told me that Marcy's daughter would be in a vacant room with a guy, two or three times a week. During the night several guys would come and go. He thinks they are dealing drugs. Marcy's daughter and a guy would quietly leave early in the morning. Sid, I had to promise him that I would keep everything strictly confidential." "Don't worry, Lucy." I said. "It's likely going to be a little complicated, but I'll think of a way to keep you completely out of this. I really appreciate you providing me with this information. Maybe it would be best if you walk around the hotel and enter through the front door. I'll wait a few minutes before going back inside the way we came. That way no one will know that you talked to me."

It was late Friday afternoon when I left Monroe for the long drive home. Heading west on US-2 the sun was already sinking in the western sky and I needed to lower the visor to keep the sun from blinding me. Near Everett I turned north on Interstate 5 and headed for Bellingham. My mind was busy assimilating the experiences of the afternoon and how to deal with the problems come Monday. Taking no action and ignoring the situation was not an option. The on-site management of the hotel was not in good hands. As managing owners we knew that our fellow owner-investors, even though they would never know about the operational details and challenges, would expect us to deal swiftly and decisively with the inexcusable behavior of the hotel manager and her daughter.

> "DECISION IS THE SPARK THAT IGNITES ACTION. UNTIL A DECISION IS MADE, NOTHING HAPPENS.... DECISION IS THE COURAGEOUS FACING OF ISSUES, KNOWING THAT IF THEY ARE NOT FACED, PROBLEMS WILL REMAIN FOREVER UNANSWERED."
>
> WILFRED A. PETERSON

Margaret could usually expect me to be home between five and five-thirty, even on the Fridays when I was in Monroe. As a result, it was understandable that she became concerned when I had still not arrived at six-thirty. Worrying about the hazards on the highway, she was very relieved when she saw me drive up and park my car in the garage. During dinner I told her an abbreviated version of the day's experiences. I have always regarded it as important to keep my wife in the loop on the events of each day. Right after dinner I called Kevin. There was no answer. When I heard the beep of the answering machine I left the following message: "Kevin, we're having a serious problem at our Monroe hotel. I'd like to pick you up at the office on Monday morning a little after nine. If that works for you, you won't need to call me. Enjoy the weekend."

Before picking up Kevin on Monday I stopped at the Baron Suites hotel in Bellingham. Without explaining the reason, I asked the manager if he could arrange to have his front desk manager drive to Monroe and have her be there at approximately 11 o'clock. He checked with her and she agreed, undoubtedly curious what it might all be about.

With Kevin driving to the Monroe hotel, I had plenty of time to brief him on the problems I had learned about the Friday before.

After parking at the hotel we immediately went to the manager's office. We were both surprised to find Marcy sitting behind the desk in the office. I didn't have to introduce Kevin since they had met before and she knew we were partners and owners. There were no friendly smiles as we settled into the two desk chairs opposite her. The sober expression on our faces may have given her a clue that "something" was serious.

"Marcy," I began while looking her sternly in the eyes, "we have enough information about both you and your daughter that had we reported it to the police there's no doubt in my mind you'd both be arrested. But we did not report it to the police. You and your daughter are both fired. We simply want you to take your belongings, have your daughter do the same, and leave the property immediately. We will go with you when you tell your daughter and we'll stay with both you and your daughter while you gather your personal items and we'll watch as you leave the property. In the event either one of you should at any time, or for any reason, return to the hotel, we'll have you both arrested." Still looking her squarely in the face I asked, "Is there any part of what I said that you do not understand?"

The blood had drained from Marcy's face. She was a large middle-aged woman. She looked scared and never said a word. We followed her as she went looking for her daughter and followed both of them as they gathered their personal items and left the property.

Moments later, Karla, the front desk manager of the Bellingham Baron Suites hotel arrived. I introduced her to Julie, the Monroe front desk agent. After some small talk I said, "Julie, I know you've seen Marcy and her daughter leave. We would like you to round up all the employees for a meeting in the Olympus room. That'll give us an opportunity to explain the reason for the departure of Marcy and her daughter." Julie asked if she should be there. "Yes Julie, Karla will take over for you while you're in the meeting."

We went to the Olympus meeting room and within a few minutes the staff members arrived. Head housekeeper Lucy walked in and looked at me nervously. She was undoubtedly worried about me spilling the secrets she had shared, even though I had promised that I would not disclose the source of the information. I told the staff, "I want to thank you all for coming. I know you're all doing a great job here and we won't keep you long. You know that Marcy has been the General Manager here since the hotel opened. Very recently we received information that both Marcy and her daughter were both involved in illegal activities. We could have informed the police and, had we done so, I have no doubt that both Marcy and her daughter would have been arrested. While we did not inform the police we had no choice other than terminating Marcy and her daughter effective immediately. We allowed them to gather their belongings and escorted them off the property with the warning that neither would be permitted to return at any time or for any reason. We regret this development but needed to take prompt and decisive action. We have applications for the manager position and believe that her replacement will soon be in place. Now we'll let you get back to work and enjoy the rest of the day. Thank you all for coming."

More projects

The Baron Inn hotel in Monroe continued to perform well and we were able to distribute good dividends to our investors every year. Because the occupancy at the hotel continued to increase, Kevin and I decided to explore how we might finance building an additional hotel in Monroe. Realtors had approached us on more than one occasion to consider selling our Bakerview Terrace apartment complex where we had significant equity. However, the financial gains would be

THE WINNER IS ALWAYS A PART OF THE ANSWER;
THE LOSER IS ALWAYS A PART OF THE PROBLEM

THE WINNER ALWAYS HAS A PLAN
THE LOSER ALWAYS HAS AN EXCUSE

THE WINNER SAYS "LET ME DO IT FOR YOU"
THE LOSER SAYS "THAT'S NOT MY JOB"

THE WINNER SEES AN ANSWER IN EVERY PROBLEM
THE LOSER SEES A PROBLEM IN EVERY ANSWER

THE WINNER SEES A GREEN NEAR EVERY SAND TRAP
THE LOSER SEES A SAND TRAP NEAR EVERY GREEN

THE WINNER SAYS "IT MAY BE DIFFICULT
BUT IT'S POSSIBLE."
THE LOSER SAYS "IT MAY BE POSSIBLE
BUT IT'S DIFFICULT."

AUTHOR UNKNOWN

taxed and the depreciation deductions would be recaptured. An alternative to an outright sale was known as a tax deferred "Starker Exchange" allowable under section 1031 of the then applicable IRS tax code. That type of transaction would allow us to transfer 100 percent of our Bakerview Terrace equity to a new hotel. We then accepted additional funds from investors and were able to purchase some land very close to the Baron Inn hotel where Exxel Pacific Construction built a beautiful Holiday Inn Express hotel. Again we were able to privately fund the entire project.

Since the two properties were virtually adjacent, we decided that one general manager would be able to oversee both and reduce overall operational costs. More than doubling the number of available hotel rooms in the small town of Monroe resulted in lowering the occupancy levels for the Baron Inn hotel. The management and operation of a hotel is much different and more complex than an apartment complex. The smooth, successful operation is dependent largely on the qualifications and quality of the general manager. We knew interviews with management applicants were very important and I always stressed the importance of treating all staff members with respect. However, there were some who believed the only way to convey managerial oversight to the staff was by saber-rattling and dictatorial behavior. Of course, this resulted in a high turn-over of employees. It was disappointing to learn that some applicants we hired did not live by the standards of behavior—integrity, honesty and responsibility—that we expected. Perhaps because we lived by those standards, without regarding ourselves as unusual or superior, we easily assumed that others would do likewise. It was painful to learn that my assumption was totally wrong after receiving a call from the Holiday Inn Express hotel one day informing me that nearly all our front desk staff had quit their jobs and would not return unless the manager was terminated. It was the most difficult management situation I had ever experienced. Fortunately I had a very reliable employee in Bellingham whose name was Brant Baron, who just happened to be one of my grandsons. Brant had worked part-time at the Baron Suites hotel from high school through Whatcom Community College. A few years later, after he graduated from the University of Washington with a degree in business administration and accounting, he became a full-time employee.

Brant was and is an exceptional young man. During the crisis situation in Monroe he worked day and night. Within a few days we hired new staff members while Brant continued to temporarily fill the role of general manager. Once a new manager was hired, Brant and I continued to visit our Monroe hotels at least once a week.

During this time, my youngest son Alan was the general manager of the Baron Suites hotel and Loren Terpstra was his assistant. They both did an exceptional job and, as a result, there were never any problems Alan and Loren couldn't handle. They had a good team of employees and very little turnover.

Brant was interested in expanding his career horizons and we began exploring the possibility of acquiring an additional hotel. Just across the street from Baron Suites was a Days Inn and almost equally close a Comfort Inn hotel. All three hotels were built around the same time. We called the owners of both properties and discovered they were willing to consider selling. I had watched the Days Inn while it was under construction and considered its quality of materials and workmanship as inferior. The Comfort Inn was about the same size as the Quality Suites. The Days Inn was the smaller of the two properties and the owner's asking price was approximately one million less than the asking price for the larger and more superior Comfort Inn. Brant did a great deal of spread sheet analyses and we concluded that the Comfort Inn offered the best likelihood of increasing in value over time. We purchased the Comfort Inn and Brant's father, my son Alan, became the manager of the new hotel as well as Baron Suites. Brant became the assistant manager of the new acquisition. A few years later I sold the Comfort Inn to Alan and Brant. With those changes, Loren Terpstra became the general manager of the Baron Suites hotel. In 2007 we sold both Monroe hotels and our investors received reasonable returns on the money they had entrusted to us. In 2011, the Baron Suites hotel was sold and I was completely out of the hotel business. Alan and Brant continued to operate the Comfort Inn very successfully.

In 1993, Kevin and I were invited to meet with three gentlemen who were planning to develop a retirement community in Lynden. The meeting was in the home of one of the interested parties who owned some land just south of town that he believed would make a good location for a retirement community project. He had already commissioned an architectural firm

> "LEADERSHIP MEANS GETTING PEOPLE TO THINK, SEE AND DO WHAT THEY MIGHT NOT HAVE DONE WITHOUT YOU. IT MEANS POSSESSING THE VISION TO SET THE RIGHT GOAL. IT MEANS BEING AWARE OF THE FEARS AND ANXIETIES FELT BY THOSE YOU LEAD EVEN AS YOU URGE THEM TO OVERCOME THOSE FEARS."
>
> BILL BRADLEY

from Minnesota to prepare the architectural plans. Since we did not know the reason for the meeting we mostly listened quietly while they showed us the plans and proposed the building site. From our seats in the living room of the man's home we were able to see the proposed building site right through his window. I mentioned that the land we were looking at was in a wetlands area near the Nooksack River and that the county government would not likely provide the permits required for construction on that site. At the same time we left no doubt that we believed having a retirement community in Lynden was very desirable. Before leaving we were asked if we were interested in becoming partners. We assured them we would give it some serious thought.

Kevin and I discussed the idea and continued meeting with the group. It was during one of the preliminary meetings that we expressed our interest in becoming partners provided the proposed building site, comprised of mostly unbuildable wetlands would no longer be considered and that a more desirable building site be acquired. The parties agreed. A partnership was formed where Kevin and I, under the Exxel Development Group, became a partner. Soon after that, a beautiful site near the rolling greens of a local golf course was purchased.

In April 1995, Exxel Pacific Construction completed the building of Meadow Greens Retirement Community and Exxel Development Group became the managing partner. We had no previous experience managing a retirement community but thought it couldn't be much different than managing an apartment complex or a hotel. We quickly learned how different it was. The residents, who were mostly retired, were very much invested in Meadow Greens because it was where they planned to stay for the rest of their lives. Unlike hotel guests or apartment dwellers, the retirement community was their home. The facility included a beautiful dining room where residents would eat three meals a day. Preparing and serving the meals required us to hire a good chef who, in turn, would hire the kitchen and dining room staff. In addition to good food the residents could enjoy the exercise room, the library, watch movies on a big screen TV or play a variety of games.

A few years later we added an additional wing to accommodate assisted-living patients. This made the management and operation of Meadow Greens more complicated. The assisted-living wing required us to employ a qualified licensed nursing staff and be able to provide assisted care services twenty-four hours a day. Needless to say, finding and employing a qualified administrator proved challenging. It made my responsibility, as one of the managing partners, more demanding since the facility also needed to comply with numerous state regulations pertaining to the care of assisted-living residents. There were times when, as managing partners, Kevin and I were involved in dealing with management problems, something the residents never knew about.

I always appreciated visiting with residents, especially those I had known for many years. Some had been my customers since the days of our retail business in Lynden.

One afternoon, as I entered the spacious lobby, I heard someone say, "Hi Sid." I recognized the man, whose name was John. He was sitting on the lobby couch visiting with two other elderly men. John had been a customer at my store for many years. Shaking his hand warmly I asked how he was doing. "Well Sid, it's been quite a few years since I bought that TV set from you. It's still working. But now that I'm in my seventies things aren't getting any better." I acknowledged that problems are common with advancing years and said, "But John, you're not that old yet." "I know, Sid, but I've never had this problem before." I asked about his problem. "Well Sid, I'll tell you," he began, "I don't care if my two friends hear it too. I know they're older but they don't have serious problems like I have. I wake up in the middle of the night cause I need to go empty my bladder. When I stand by the toilet it won't come. Instead it just drips a little. My goodness I could stand there all night. Drip, drip, drip. Sid it's plain awful." Then Bill, who was sitting next to John pipes up. "John you think that's bad, I'm in my eighties and my problem is worse than yours. I go sit on the toilet for a bowel movement. I push. I grunt and groan, grunt and groan. Nothing comes. It's just terrible." Immediately Ken, who is sitting on the right next to Bill, chimed in. "Yes, you guys have problems but mine is a lot worse. I just turned ninety and I'm in good shape. The problem is that my wife Hazel won't let me sleep with her anymore. That's because at six o'clock I have no trouble emptying my bladder. At seven o'clock I have a healthy bowel movement." Almost in unison, John and Bill ask: "Ken what in the world are you bellyaching about?" Putting his head down Ken said, "I don't wake up until seven-thirty."

As of the time of this writing, Kevin and I are still the managing partners of Meadow Greens Retirement Community.

***

Epilogue

Those interested in successfully starting and/or operating a business have hopefully found some ideas or inspiration from this book. Others may be wondering if starting a small business can still lead to the level of achievement you've been reading about. Let me assure you that during my many years of struggling to succeed, I never expected the achievements I've been blessed to enjoy. Through my entire career I never quit dreaming. I still believe that America is the land of unlimited opportunity. While I understand some government regulations are absolutely necessary, many are no longer required. If excessive and unnecessary regulations begin to choke the entrepreneurial spirit and diminish opportunity, it could lead to the end of the free enterprise system; the foundation of the greatness in America.

It was in the 1980s when Kevin DeVries and I formed a partnership which has stood the test of time. Statistically 80 percent of business partnerships fail within a few years. Over 70 percent of those failed partnerships end up in court. Most have painful outcomes. Those statistics are worse than the percentages of failed marriages and divorces. Often I have asked myself: What are the ingredients that made our partnership last for thirty years and counting?

When Kevin and I first started Exxel Pacific Construction we could not have known that thirty years later our company would be among the largest private companies in Washington state. Nor could we have known that the company would directly employ over 100 professionals in the construction industry (and vendors whose employment runs into the thousands). When we started we could not have dreamed that the company would have a fleet of aircraft making it possible for project managers and others to visit their various job sites at least once a week and still be home to spend evenings with their families. Nor could we have known that the company would gain the expertise to build huge skyscrapers.

During its first years our company grew slowly. Experienced employees were added. Costly mistakes were made. An ongoing challenge always was (and still is) to convey to our leadership team members the importance of never forgetting the values and principles upon which the company was founded.

In September 1998 we decided to take our Exxel Pacific employees and their families on the second annual retreat at the beautiful ski resort in Whistler, B.C. During the time of both fun and fellowship we also held meetings that company employees were required to attend. As the then President of the company I addressed the assembled group with the following speech:

> "A year ago, during our first annual Whistler retreat, I talked about Exxel Pacific; its strengths, but also its weaknesses. Since then Exxel Pacific has become a stronger company. Today I want to talk about the future of Exxel. Where will Exxel be five, ten, twenty or fifty years from now? Will it make transitions from one generation, from one administration to the next without upheaval? For some time now, I have busied myself in a quest to learn what the ingredients are that cause some companies to thrive, flourish and prosper from one generation to the next while others fail.
>
> "Most Whatcom County general contractors will not last beyond the current generation. Why do some survive while most do not? Not only did I examine companies within the realm of my own experience, I also studied some of the great corporations within some of the world's giant industries. What I found is that it is not WHAT a company does. It's NOT that they never change. It's NOT that they had lofty goals and a strategic plan. In fact, some didn't know exactly what they wanted to do when they started in business. Like Bill and Dave. When they opened a little shop in Dave's

garage over fifty years ago all they had was $538.00 in cash. They didn't know what they were going to make or how they were going to sell it. But they had strong principles and they knew HOW they wanted to conduct their business. Not only were they committed to providing their customers the best in quality and value, they were equally committed to providing their employees the opportunity to build pleasant rewarding careers. That was their vision. Did they succeed? Bill and Dave's vision, over the past five decades created a company valued at 31 billion dollars with more than 100,000 employees! I'll bet most people are using at least one of this company's products. Yes, it's Hewlett-Packard.

"To survive that long, a company must constantly protect its health. Can you imagine the enormous changes in the life of an organization that has survived for 100 years or longer? Imagine the enormous changes it has encountered. To live that long a company must have a 'soul' in the form of a set of central, core values that transcend generations of personnel, administrations and constant change. To live that long a company must have a noble reason for existence. The 'soul' of a company is one of those concepts that, like beauty, evaporates when you try to define it. But, like beauty, it is instantly recognizable. It is an ingredient that is easily picked up by others including personnel, clients, suppliers and, yes, even competitors. It manifests in the form of Energy,

Enthusiasm, Excitement, Effort and Excellence. There is a sense that the business, and all those associated with it, fulfills a meaningful role in society. A business that aims for something larger than just making money. A company that is enriched by the commitment, the skills, the contribution and values of every individual that is associated with it. A company that would never ask a marketing specialist or consultant to write its mission or vision statement because that would be like asking a stranger to identify them. But there are companies and organizations who do exactly that. These are places where humans are viewed as machines, dedicated only to productivity and efficiency. They are, in my opinion, companies without a soul.

"Some are aware that I'm not a great advocate of conventional, 'in the box' forms of strategic planning like that taught in business schools and presented by banks and investors as an absolutely essential ingredient for a growing company. I believe conventional strategic planning is usually implemented by aspiring entrepreneurs who have no experience, possess little vision and zero creativity.

"I'm not the only who believes this. Here is what business research specialists Collins and Porras found in their research of the largest and most successful companies:

"'In examining the history of successful companies, we were struck by how often they make their best moves not by detailed strategic planning, but rather by experimentation, trial and error, sometimes accident, but more often, jumping on opportunities when they present themselves. In hindsight, they often look like the result of a brilliant company strategy. If top management lacks the vision to recognize meritorious or promising opportunities when they present themselves, no amount of strategic planning will cover such deficiencies.'

"In my talk last year I spoke briefly about the values our company embraces and holds dear. I used words such as honesty, integrity, and quality.

"But they are only words. What they really mean has been my credo in every business I've started. They are the guiding principles that can lead Exxel Pacific to greatness. If they become the fundamental essence of the people that make up the company (YOU!) then Exxel Pacific will truly have a long bright prosperous future where the torch of its core values is passed from one generation, and from one management team, to the next.

"A company CEO once asked a few new prospective employees what they thought was the purpose of the company.

"One said: 'To make money.'

"Another said: 'To make our customers happy.'

"Still another responded: 'To make our owners happy.'

"The last one said: 'To produce top quality work.'

"The CEO responded saying, 'The purpose of this company is to enable all of us to have wonderfully fulfilling lives. In order to do that we have to work our guts out for the customer, keep our suppliers and fellow team members happy, and do wonderful high-quality work. In that order.

"Exxel Pacific is a company comprised of men and women who are dedicated to serve the best interest of the client at all times. Men and women who care about the well-being of their families, who respect their fellow employees and regard them as members of their extended families.

"We are men and women who understand that each has a responsibility in life to be a contributing, productive citizen in our society and a positive influence in the life of others.

"Men and women who:

- Embrace the highest aspirations for personal achievement and fulfillment.
- Understand that the company could not offer meaningful employment to anyone, or provide services for any clients, if it is not operated successfully and profitably.
- Individually share a measure of responsibility for the success and profitability of the company and embrace our company mission to deliver exceptional value to our customers.

- Are able to assume a measure of responsibility for the integrity and reputation of the company.

  "Subscribing to our core values are essential for employment in Exxel Pacific. It is also an inflexible requirement for anyone in management, or aspiring to be in management, at Exxel. Those violating or compromising our core values will not have long term tenure at this company.

  "Let's look at some specific scenarios in the workplace that are not acceptable:

- Negative attitudes.

  "Negative attitudes are like a contagious virus, capable of destroying not only the individual who harbors them, they can also infect others in the workplace.

  "Sharing negative attitudes with fellow team members is like spreading a hideous poison. A person unable to control a predisposition to negative attitudes will not be a long term Exxel team member.

- Taking advantage of customers, subcontractors or suppliers is no more acceptable than allowing customers, suppliers or subcontractors to take advantage of Exxel.
- Those who repeatedly, in their area of responsibility, fail to do the right thing, or those who repeatedly demonstrate their inability to do their job right, cannot long be members of this company's team

member family. No company can be the best, unless its people are the best.

"Remember, doing the right thing also demands that we're doing things right.

"A few years ago we had a reputation of enormous kindness and generosity among employees and sub-contractors. At the time we were on the threshold of bankruptcy. Without intervention we would not exist today. It may have seemed that we were doing the right thing, but we were clearly not doing it right. Let me give you four reasons why Exxel Pacific could fail to be a long lasting visionary company:

1. If the leadership fails to subscribe to a company core ideology, is not committed to the long haul and is simply wanting to make a lot of money, cash out and retire.
2. If the leadership does not have a drive for progress with a constant urge to continue improving and moving forward.
3. If the leadership isn't interested in a values-driven company with a sense of purpose beyond just making money.
4. If the leadership doesn't care about building a lasting company that will be strong only both during their tenure and for decades beyond.

"Other than for those four reasons you can expect Exxel to be a dynamic, growing company far into the unforeseeable future.

"I've started a number of small businesses. I believe that all are in existence today, providing employment to many, while growing and thriving. All came to be successful because the core values I've discussed are an integral part of me and of the companies I founded. Long ago I learned that for a company to succeed in the long run, the company must be guided by something that is larger and nobler than any of us. Each succeeding year of learning and experience re-enforces that. So, my friends, when you reach the mature age of sixty-eight, remind yourself that learning never stops.

"Why should I, at a mature age, still be so excited about Exxel Pacific Construction? I've never been particularly motivated by money or wealth because they only determine one measure of success. Feeding a huge ego has never been a driving force, either. The fact that I'm excited about this company is the very reason why you should be excited about it.

"I have a vision of what this company, with people like you and others like you, can be.

"It is company with unlimited opportunities. Where every team member enjoys having a part in building the biggest and most reputable construction company in the state. A company where every team member has appropriated, with his or her own principles, the core values of the company.

"A company where someday your children may like to work because they heard from Mom or Dad that Exxel Pacific is a company that does the right thing. A company that does it right!

"To continue our growth we must answer this question: How can we continue to attract the caliber of top notch people that can help Exxel Pacific grow? Within the next few months I will, for exploration and discussion purposes, present to the management committee a proposed program that would make it possible for qualified Exxel team members to purchase shares of ownership in the company. I believe it is going to be a key ingredient in attracting additional highly-skilled, qualified entrepreneurial professionals. Especially as this company continues to grow and the demand for skilled construction professionals remains high, it could give us a recruiting edge. It will appeal to those who are ambitious, are eager to assume full responsibility for their own success and be instrumental in the success of the company. That is the caliber of people who will help Exxel Pacific achieve greatness.

"What is the future of Exxel Pacific? Where will the company be five or ten years from now? What do I see in the 'crystal ball?' You would hardly recognize it! You might look at a huge high-rise structure and proudly say 'Exxel Pacific Construction built it.' What will be the total volume of business? Provided, this company succeeds in attracting additional competent quality people and never loses track of or compromises the core values we've talked about, then there is virtually no limit to its growth. In addition, all of you who have helped make the present exciting will likely be a part of our exciting future.

"I've long understood that one will never be able to achieve that which one's dreams cannot conceive. The first steps to extraordinary achievement are visualization and dreaming. Already, at the age of fifteen I was a 'dreamer.' That is how I have been able to build several successful companies. Now let's dream together. Let us constantly rekindle the fire of our imagination. Then, for you and your family, the greatest material fulfillment will be that you have played a part in building a company that competitors will attempt to imitate. But they will never be able to duplicate what we've done because they don't have YOU! That's how we will together build Exxel Pacific.

"I have long pondered the question: What are the ingredients that have made our partnership successful and, in fact, are essential for any partnership to be successful?

"Lasting partnerships are built on a strong foundation of core principles which the partners must agree on both personally and professionally. Kevin and I had a common bond of faith and values. Sharing a common bond is key to any partnership. It's what will keep you and your partner(s) in it for the long-run. In our partnership we believe in treating our employees like family and in treating our customers with the utmost respect, honesty and integrity. Often entrepreneurs enter into a partnership with unrealistic and unspoken expectations that can later sabotage the relationship.

"IF YOU DON'T GO AFTER WHAT YOU WANT, YOU'LL NEVER HAVE IT. IF YOU DON'T ASK, THE ANSWER IS ALWAYS NO. IF YOU DON'T STEP FORWARD, YOU'LL ALWAYS BE IN THE SAME PLACE."

NORA ROBERTS

"You have undoubtedly read a number of books and publications dealing with starting, operating, and organizing a business along with the various ingredients that will help your business thrive. Nearly all business books deal with the importance of setting goals. One article I read recently was the story of an active entrepreneur. His goal was being one of the world's billionaires before he reached the age of thirty. Reading the background of the entrepreneur I was certain that he was setting himself up for massive disappointments. I'm not opposed to setting goals that are realistic and achievable. That said, it is important to understand that by making your goals achievable, and after preparing a list of steps that you and your partner agree on, you then take the various little steps to achieve until you reach your goal. You should also envision possible 'setbacks' and what you might need to do to survive should you be assaulted by the worst of 'Murphy's Laws.' Though I'm not opposed to setting goals, neither am I a strong advocate either. After Exxel Pacific had become reasonably successful, I remember a board meeting where the merit of setting goals was brought up. One of the board members suggested setting a goal of growing the company to a maximum of $25 million in annual revenue. That set off my belief in unlimited opportunity and prompted me to ask: "Why would we want to set a ceiling? What would we do if we had opportunities to exceed that lofty achievement? Now, several years later, the company has broken through the ceiling several times simply by adhering to its mission statement:

"We are committed to proactively satisfy our customers by providing the most cost-efficient and high-quality projects in our area of service. This is achieved by building a team of people who will develop and maintain a quality, service and solution-oriented attitude that will lead the industry and create a sustainable competitive advantage for Exxel Pacific, Inc.

> "We all pledge the highest level of integrity and accountability to the pursuit of excellence in everything we do and that our subcontractors and suppliers do for us."

It was at the occasion of Exxel Pacific's annual Christmas party in 2011 years after responsibilities of being the president of the company had been turned over to my friend and partner, Kevin DeVries. I was simply the Chairman of the Board and a minority shareholder. But my pride in the company that Kevin and I founded never diminished. Again I had the privilege of addressing the company's employees and their spouses. Before speaking I looked out at the large group of people. Nearly all were professionals comprised of project managers, project superintendents, project engineers, and other specialists and executives. The company had grown at least ten-fold since my earlier speech.

> "Ladies and gentlemen, because there are so many new faces here I would like tell you just a little about the early beginnings of your company.
>
> "It was after my friend and partner Kevin DeVries successfully completed all the details involved in overseeing a construction company building our Bakerview Terrace Apartment complex that we began dreaming about starting our own construction company. While all accomplishments in life begin with an idea, we could never have imagined what Exxel Pacific would be like so many years later. Yes, there are serious risks in

starting any new business. We experienced near failure more than once. Each in our own way, Kevin and I prayed. There are times in everyone's life where we deal with problems that are bigger and more powerful than any one of us. *Psychology Today* said that those who don't believe in a higher power may need to invent one. Survival and success in a company is accomplished by teamwork. There are many of you I do not personally know and many of you do not personally know me. But as I look over the crowd gathered here tonight, I am grateful and appreciative that you are all members of the Exxel team. I especially appreciate that you all know the values which formed the foundation of Exxel Pacific Construction from its beginning. Those values are based on the Christian principles of honesty and integrity. Of treating employees, customers, competitors and subcontractors with respect, with caring and with dignity. As members of our company team, all of you have your areas of responsibility. Many of you have positions of leadership. Leaders become great. Not because of their power, but because of their ability to motivate and empower others. I read a letter a few days ago that made me proud of the Exxel team. Let me share with you an abbreviated version of that letter.

"I'm a homeowner in Seattle where Exxel Pacific is building a project. I have been around construction projects for many years in various roles. I would like to commend your project management team for having the absolutely, hands down, best and safest construction site I have ever seen. I can safely assume that every aspect of the building is 'top-notch.' As I drive by every evening after work I'm always impressed with the attention to safety, signage, traffic control and cleanliness of the site. It is amazing."

"If you continue to succeed with those leadership qualities, Exxel Pacific will continue to grow and flourish and be the pride of you and every member of the Exxel team.

"We can influence others more by the conduct of our lives than by the messages of our words."

QUESTIONS AND ANSWERS

Q Is your relationship with employees important?

A Yes, very much so, and here is an example: There were several people milling around as I entered the lobby of Meadow Greens Retirement Community, which I own together with my partner, Kevin, and serve as managing partner. Just then a tall, distinguished-looking gentleman with graying hair approached me. He clasped my hand, shook it warmly and said, "Sid, do you remember me?" As we shook, while looking in his face, recognition slowly surfaced and then suddenly I knew. "John DeWit," I said while shaking his hand anew. "John, tell me about your life." We sat down as John began. "Sid, it's been so many years since you hired me to work in your radio station. At the time I was a high school student. Currently I live in Florida with my wife and mostly grown children. I travel all over the world in conjunction with my job helping universities utilize technology in their curriculum." I listened with admiration to this former youthful employee who clearly had become a success in life. "Sid," John continued, "you have no idea how often I've talked about you while addressing college and university students in various countries around the world." I looked at John thinking he could read the disbelieving expression on my face. "Sid, you were the first person to hire me. During that time in my life I was skeptical because I had come to believe that business people did not have a good reputation. To this day I'm not sure why I thought that. "My dad was a dairy farmer and may have had an unpleasant experience dealing with businesspeople. As a child I remember overhearing conversations about his negative experience with a certain business. I might have subliminally concluded that businessmen were not to be trusted. It was with that sense of prejudice that I came to work for you."

> "IN BUSINESS WE LEARN HOW TO MAKE MONEY. WE MUST LEARN HOW TO LIVE A LIFE OF MEANING."
>
> SID BARON

I had been listening quietly and thoughtfully as John, looking me straight in the face, continued. "Sid I knew you were a very busy man because you were running both the store and the radio station. However, on more than one occasion you took the time to sit down and talk with me. You asked questions about what I expected to accomplish in my life and took a personal interest in me. It impressed me and I've never forgotten that. You were not initially concerned about what I could do for you. Instead you were interested in me as a person and made me think about my future." Other than thanking him for his kind words, I didn't know what to say to John. I had no recollection of private conversations with him or any of the many high school students that worked for me part time. This incident clearly crystalized in my mind that, as employers, how we treat our employees, our young people, and others is vitally important. What we say to encourage or discourage can be a powerful influencing factor for the rest of their lives.

Q How did you handle terminating employees?

A Firing an employee is unpleasant both for the person being terminated and the "terminator." In business, unfortunately, there are times when it is necessary to end a relationship with an employee. During my long business career I can remember only two occasions that I had to fire an employee on the spot. Once I walked past the desk of our receptionist who, at the time, was talking on the telephone to a customer. She had not seen me approach and seemed to be concentrating on some paperwork. When I overheard her uttering profane words I stopped in my track and waited for her to finish the conversation. When she noticed me standing there the conversation with the client stopped quickly. Without raising my voice I calmly said: "Rhonda, I'm sure you know that your language just now while talking to a client was entirely inappropriate. "I'm sorry", she murmured. "Rhonda,

I'm going to have to let you go immediately." While gathering her belongings she said, "I understand," and walked out of the front door while dabbing tears from her eyes.

I have also had to terminate employees for serious reasons including stealing, sexual harassment and more. In these cases, my approach was pretty direct. I would call him or her into my office and advise the employee that the purpose of the meeting would be "termination" of employment. Time spent counseling an employee was far more meaningful than using harsh words and attacking a person's self-esteem. We always parted with a handshake while expressing my belief that the person would never repeat the offenses that led to his or her dismissal.

Q What do you believe are the essential ingredients for success in business?

A A strong desire to be your own boss. You must be predisposed with that desire rather than developing that desire because you happen to be working for a boss you either don't like or don't respect. To succeed you must have a passion to be successful no matter how long or hard you need to work. It also helps to choose a business in a field where you know that you will enjoy the work. Whatever business activity you choose, expect unforeseen changes. Something that's in great demand today may not be tomorrow. That's especially true in the field of technology. You must be flexible, nimble and quick to adapt. In my experience, selling expensive electronic organs at one time was a very profitable area of my retail business. Many people purchased one to be used as a family fun center. One morning I received a notice from the Thomas Organ Company that they had discontinued manufacturing electronic organs. They had accurately foreseen that inexpensive keyboards, computers, video games and other developments represented a huge change in the marketplace. The advantage of being small makes it much easier to change course than it is for huge companies. If you feel you could benefit from a boost in creativity and brainstorming you might visit the website innovationtools.com which focuses on business innovation.

Q **Is starting my own business risky?**

A Becoming your own boss does not guarantee success. Therefore you need to be willing to take risks with your own money and your security. You should not take those risks if you don't have complete confidence in yourself and your ability to succeed. If you think that owning your own business is a nine-to-five job, you'll never succeed. Early in my business career I became a firm believer in bootstrapping. It made me work harder without dealing with the pressure of having to pay back money borrowed from friends and/or family. Yes, attempting to start your own business is risky. You need an abundance of self-confidence without being "cocky" or arrogant. You also need to be brutally honest with yourself when you make a list of all the things that could go wrong. If you're not comfortable with risking the possibility of failure, ***don't start.*** You should never be reluctant to seek advice from experienced people whom you respect. If you fear that asking for advice from an experienced person will result in hearing things you may not want to hear, then ***don't start.***

Q Can you identify other characteristics to evaluate before proceeding with my plans to become my own boss?

A Look deeply into your very being and answer the following questions:

- Do you tire easily or possess boundless energy?
- Are you willing to risk your own money and your economic security?
- Do you have the skills required to inspire others?
- Are you determined, enthusiastic and strong-willed?
- Do you give up easily or do you have "never, never give up determination"?
- Do you consider yourself both capable and competitive in your undertakings?
- Are you likely to consider a failure as fatal or merely a stepping stone to success?
- Are you persistent? Can you live with the thought "if at first I don't succeed, I'll try, try again?"

Many people who want to be entrepreneurs don't realize that they do not possess the requisite ingredients. They often mistakenly believe that they need reams of paper to prepare financial projections, feasibility and market studies. However, without prior experience it is virtually impossible to determine how all the studies and projections will translate to the real world. If your business plan is new and innovative your projections are likely to be of little value. Once you've turned your entrepreneurial passion into a successful beginning you may well need investors to grow your enterprise. That's when you need a business plan, market studies, financial projections and a ream of paper.

Q Did your busy business life allow you to spend adequate time with your children?

A That was a pressure point in my life. I loved my wife and children more than anything and often felt guilty about not spending enough time with them. Sunday afternoons were the time to spend some enjoyable time with my four growing sons. Often we'd have bicycle races on our quiet country road. That was until the day came when they'd win every race. We would also go to a small densely wooded area in the back of our forty-acre farm and play hide and seek. Those were precious hours of bonding with my children. We were blessed that Margaret was an exceptional mother who took great pride in her children. They were always dressed neatly for school or church and she was able to deal with the challenges of childhood naughtiness and disobedience. On the rare occasions that serious disciplinary action was called for, she'd wait until I came home to discuss the issues and we'd agree on the appropriate punishment. As a result, our children knew that they would never be able to "play one parent against the other."

Q Is being passionate about a specific activity sufficient reason to pursue it as a business opportunity?

A To become (or remain) successful by focusing only on money isn't good. The focus has to be on the larger purpose of what you are doing and why you are doing it. Your chances for success will increase by looking at where you want to go and what you would like your legacy to be. Understand that there is no "instant gratification" when you are running your own business. You won't get a paycheck every month like you do in a forty-hour-per-week job. For a period of time, you may need to work very hard with little, if any, monetary reward.

Remember, your life as an entrepreneur will not always be fun. You must have realistic expectations and measure your success not only in financial terms but also through satisfaction with life as a whole. Happiness does not come from a headlong charge toward wealth. It is about finding satisfaction in yourself and in what you have done.

Ask yourself these fundamental questions:

How do you really want to live your life?

What do you want to accomplish in your life?

It has been a few years since I read Stephen Covey's popular book *The Seven Habits of Highly Effective People.* In one chapter, "Begin with the End in Mind," he recommends formulating a "personal vision statement" to document one's own vision for life. Since I already strongly subscribed to that concept, I did not do what he recommended, which was to write a personal mission statement. I recommend that you do that only after you seriously visualize the day when you die. What do you want your loved ones and friends to say or remember about you?

Q How did you deal with jealousy or other conflicts among employees?

A Jealousy in the workplace is not uncommon. Lack of recognition or selectively praising some staff or team members by a manager can easily result in jealousy. Praising all employees for a job well done instead of just a select few will reduce jealousy and conflict. Everyone likes to know that the boss thinks they are doing a good job and that they are appreciated. In the hotel business there are two primary departments:

1. The front desk and office operations.
2. The housekeeping and laundry operations.

Front desk and office personnel generally receive slightly more compensation. They are required to have good communication skills as well as being proficient on the computer—something not required for housekeeping and laundry personnel. This easily makes some employees feel inferior to others. I always made it a priority to point out that the two departments were equally important for the successful operation of the hotel. That success was attributable to the housekeeping staff keeping the rooms in excellent condition and gave the front desk staff the enthusiasm to keep rooms occupied with satisfied guests. All employees were equally important and the general manager was required to treat all employees with equal respect.

Q You wrote that during your business career you barely avoided bankruptcy. Can you give any specifics?

A When I received my license from the Federal Communications Commission to operate radio station KLYN-FM in November 1960, I had no experience in the business of operating a commercial broadcast station. As a result, I did not know that I couldn't play recorded music without paying fees. That changed when a couple of well-dressed "inspectors" walked in late one Friday afternoon. They introduced themselves as enforcement officers for ASCAP (American Society of Composers, Authors and Publishers). I knew I was not knowingly guilty of having done anything illegal. The gentlemen explained that ASCAP was in charge of collecting royalty fees on any copyrighted material which included the recorded music we were broadcasting. I was informed that I had not paid the fees for nearly three years. They did not accept my explanation that I had been unaware of this requirement and insisted that I pay them immediately for all past due fees. That was a considerable amount and I told them that I was struggling to keep the radio station operating and simply did not have the money to pay. They closed their books and informed me that they would file a lawsuit. I was staring at the floor and remained silent for nearly a minute. Then I raised my head and looking them squarely in the eyes said: "Gentlemen, I understand the legal requirement to pay those fees on a monthly basis and starting this month I can promise you that I will never miss a payment. I can also tell you that as soon as I'm served with your lawsuit I will turn off the big switch on the station transmitter and KLY-FM will be off the air. When the time comes I will be happy to tell the judge that I had agreed to pay the monthly fees from this day forward and why I had no choice but to discontinue the operation of my much-listened-to broadcast station." After a moment of silence, they asked to discuss the matter between themselves privately. I excused myself until one of the gentlemen came out of the office and asked me to join them again. One of the men said: "Mr. Baron, we have no doubt about your sincerity and no desire to inflict financial distress on you and the radio station. We believe that from now on you will pay the fees regularly and with that promise we will forgive all the past due fees and forget about a lawsuit." I thanked the gentlemen. We shook hands and they departed.

There was another close call which could have resulted in the death of my business. This came during the time of Motivating Sound Inc., when we were manufacturing and distributing background music systems. One of our customers, who was an electronic engineer working for a Salem, Oregon, based company, also lived in Salem. His firm had designed one of the first solid-state portable transceivers. Their first production run was purchased by the State Forest Department. Unfortunately for the company, the units had a transistor overheating problem which rendered them unusable within a short period of time. The Salem design and manufacturing facility was owned by a larger company located in Minnesota. They suffered major losses and decided to discontinue their design and production of portable transistorized transceivers. Instead they decided, under the direction of their engineer, Mr. Marr, to develop and manufacture electronic merchandising systems. Mr. Marr was our background music dealer in the Salem area and I had come to know him well. He had told me about his employer proceeding with the electronic merchandising units and was approaching the assembly phase. Then one morning I received a phone call from Mr. Marr. "Sid, the Minnesota company has decided to pull the plug on the Salem operation and they want to dump all their partially-assembled units. I was thinking this would be a great opportunity for your company to acquire the inventory and expand your product line." I told him that I was very interested in such an exceptional opportunity but was sure I could not afford it. He explained that the Minnesota company was eager to close the factory and two of the company's executives would be coming in the following Monday. I agreed to meet with them to discuss the possibility of making a deal. After all, entrepreneurs are calculated risk takers. But as I piloted my single engine four seat Piper back toward Bellingham I encountered deteriorating weather. The aviation map on my knees was of little help in navigating since visibility was poor and I was not equipped to fly solely by aircraft instruments. As long as I remained northbound while flying above Interstate Highway 5, I knew I was heading in the right direction. To keep the freeway in sight I had to gradually decrease my altitude to 1000 feet, which is the lowest legal altitude allowed while flying over populated areas. The forward visibility was virtually down to zero and I was getting nervous. Suddenly a voice from the radio crackled: "Chehalis radio this is Cessna November 6890 Echo position report. Two miles north of Chehalis southbound over I-5 at 1000 feet." At a combined closing speed of nearly 300 miles per hour I was on a direct collision course with an oncoming aircraft which I could not see. There was no time to think. Immediately I made a left turn knowing that the Chehalis airport was west of the Interstate. To my immense relief the airport runway was right in front and below me. I pulled the power, lowered the flaps and landed on the wet runway.

After taxiing to the airport office I made arrangements to rent a car for the more than three hour drive to Lynden. I was grateful to be alive after such a close call. Soon my thoughts returned to the big factory inventory purchase. I had the uneasy feeling that my excitement about the possibilities had obscured my fear of failure. I knew we were seriously undercapitalized and should have known that what I was trying to accomplish would require a great deal of money. I did have six months to pay for the inventory and had we not had collection problems with some of our key distributors, I might have succeeded. Now our total debt exceeded our total assets and we were heading for bankruptcy. Most of our debts were from the unpaid balance we owed the Minnesota firm for their Salem inventory. The attorney representing the Minnesota firm was very aggressive in his efforts to collect. When I received a registered letter informing me of a pending lawsuit I knew we would lose. I spent most of that day composing a response letter to the attorney. In it I was very honest advising the attorney that if the legal action proceeded, I would have to immediately declare bankruptcy. I respectfully requested that our company be allowed to return the merchandise, most of which we still had in our warehouse. Fortunately the attorney accepted. He most likely understood that if we filed for bankruptcy he would not get any money nor any merchandise returned. It was a close call I never wanted to experience again.

Q Did you ever begin planning your estate?

A During the first thirty years of my business career I didn't have much of an estate to think about. By the age of about fifty that began to change when I experienced the satisfaction of starting businesses that became successful and began to bring financial rewards. I did not know to what extent the incurable disease multiple sclerosis would affect my life expectancy. It was undoubtedly a factor in my decision to take my estate planning seriously. My accountant advised me that taxes would take most of our estate at the time of our departure from this mortal life unless I did some creative planning. I studied a great deal about estate planning and learned that it would not entirely eliminate estate taxes. However, I could take steps to make sure that our family and our favorite charities would be the primary beneficiaries of my estate. After researching charitable foundations, I engaged the services of a Seattle law firm to establish the Baron Foundation. Our wills were then rewritten stipulating that our six children would each receive a certain amount as their inheritance. The entire remainder of the estate, if any, would be donated to the Baron Foundation to be gifted to the charities Margaret and I had identified. As the value of our estate continued to grow, we decided to designate two of our income producing properties to be owned by an entity named the Sid and Margaret Baron LLC. This was specifically established to allow parents to annually gift unit shares in the LLC to their children in the amount allowed under IRS rules and limits. As the Managing Member of the LLC, I remained completely responsible for every aspect in the operation of the properties. The profits generated by the LLC-owned properties were distributed annually according to the children's and grandchildren's percentage of ownership. Since additional unit shares were gifted to our children, the annual dividends paid also increased commensurate with their increasing ownership percentages. When in 2011 and 2012 I decided to sell the properties, the proceeds of the sales were distributed to our family members consistent with their respective percentages of ownership. Margaret and I have enjoyed being able to give parts of our estate to our children and grandchildren while we are still in the land of the living.

Q Do you still believe that America is the land of unlimited opportunity?

A It has been our family tradition for many years to get together with our entire family around Christmas time. As I write this it's late in December 2012. All sixty-five members, including the great grandchildren, of the Sid and Margaret Baron family are together at the Holiday Inn hotel in Everett, WA. To begin my response to the question I want to tell you about my conversation this morning with one of my grandsons in-law. His name is Jeremy Crossin and he is married to my granddaughter Lindsay. They live in the Boston area where Jeremy is employed as an equipment technician for a pharmaceutical company. Early in life Jeremy knew that he wanted to "get ahead." Through positive reenforcement by his dad he knew he could achieve what most would consider impossible. He wanted to "rise above the crowd" and also learned that his young wife Lindsay, my granddaughter, had similar drive and ambitions. Jeremy knew that one essential ingredient in becoming successful is to have the ability and discipline to save a little money every month. Doing this made it possible for them to buy their first home and very recently, after moving to the Boston area, adding a duplex. Their home, located in the eastern part of Washington State, is being rented with the monthly rental income substantially larger than their monthly mortgage payment. Now they will be living in the upstairs of their duplex and renting the other half. Jeremy and Lindsay, at a very young age, are already proving that America still is the land of unlimited opportunity.

Q Are there still opportunities to start a small business with little money?

A Driving through a largely residential area in the Fairhaven district of Bellingham I noticed a neon sign in the window of a residence which read "Computer Repair." Computer repair and upgrading is a forty billion dollar business and growing. If you're not already a computer expert you might have to take a home study course just like I did many years ago in television and radio electronic servicing. Then you need to get out among people and solicit their business. The face-to-face personal contact is very effective and handing your prospective client one of your business cards is much less expensive than placing newspaper ads.

"EARNED SUCCESS IS THE IDEA THAT YOU'RE CREATING VALUE WITH YOUR LIFE AND VALUE IN THE LIVES OF OTHERS."

MARVIN OLASKY

There are a plethora of other opportunities for the would-be entrepreneurs such as starting a tutorial center on any subject in which the person is knowledgeable. Many businesses can be started on a shoestring such as building websites, computer repair, wedding photography, event planning and many others. In the days of my youth I could not have dreamed about computers, the Internet, E-mail, cell phones and so many other technological developments. We could no longer function in our businesses without those developments any more than we could function in our homes without electricity.

"LEADERS BECOME GREAT, NOT BECAUSE OF THEIR POWER BUT BECAUSE OF THEIR ABILITY TO MOTIVATE AND EMPOWER OTHERS."

SID BARON

In the final analyses faith, family and friends form the foundation of our existence.

The value of our lives and its fulfillment are not measured by the accumulation of wealth but what we do for others throughout the journey.

I recommend you keep a gratitude journal. Sit down, daily, and write about the things for which you are grateful. Start with whatever springs to mind and work from there. Try not to write the same thing every day but instead explore your gratefulness.

ADDENDUM

How I became a successful investor in the stock market. Many investors, even those who have been active in the stock market for many years, give up trading after suffering losses. With the arrival of computers, the Internet and online trading, you may be thinking about trying again. After all, it is now possible to trade in the stock market without having to pay hefty commissions to a broker. Rather than following the advice of a broker you can do your own research and select the most promising stocks. There is a plethora of research material available on the Internet these days. There are also newsletters published by so-called experts recommending a portfolio of winning stocks. But, even with all the research and ease of trading, you may still find yourself to be among the 80 percent of investors who still lose money.

In my many years of investing, I've been there and completely understand your dilemma.

My online investing learning curve started in 1998 when I was still involved in managing my other businesses. After mailing a $5,000 check to Datek Online it was time to begin learning about investing using my own computer. Sometime later, Datek Online either was purchased or merged with Ameritrade. I've used the Ameritrade trading platform ever since. Shortly after mailing my $5,000 account opening check I added $50,000 to my trading account. For the purpose of walking through the learning curve with me I am going to assume that the reader has $50,000 available for investing. I'm also assuming that the reader knows that there are no investments that I know of which are completely without risk. Especially during the first few years of learning I often lost money on some investments. You will learn that, over time, I learned to employ a strategy that minimized the possibility and amount of losses. While it is not possible to eliminate all risks it is possible to reduce the investor's risks to acceptable levels.

It is common knowledge that many beginner investors start trading after the stock market has been climbing week after week and month after month (much like lottery ticket buyers make their purchases when lottery pools reach record levels). They can't help hearing some of their friends or acquaintances bragging about the money they're making in the stock market. Or else they'll hear about some company that's fabulously successful and their friends, who purchased its stock, are making a bundle. Often that's a good enough "tip" for them to jump in and invest their hard-earned savings in that "fabulously successful"company. Then, just when they think all is well, the uninformed investor all of a sudden learns that a big chunk of their hard-earned savings is lost.

Here is why that approach to investing is almost a certain formula for failure.

- During its history, the stock market has been characterized by many peaks and valleys. These ups and downs can happen dramatically in a single day. Even an experienced investor can never know with certainty when the market has reached a peak. Conversely, when the market has been on a downward slide, the bottom can never be accurately predicted.
- The uninformed beginner investor should never invest because they heard about a certain company stock from a friend.
- As an investor you should never "put all your eggs in one basket." I'm a firm believer in diversification. I have practiced that, not only in the stock market but in the various business entities I've started throughout my long business career.
- Research is very important and when you get finished with this section you will have learned that it's not complicated.

How I got started

I'm writing this primarily because if you are interested in being successful in the stock market you can avoid all the mistakes and missteps I made before learning how to get on the right track. During my research I subscribed to Investment Newsletters, attended seminars and money shows in Las Vegas and listened to experts in various fields. In addition to acquiring a library of books, I subscribed to a service where an "expert" would augment monthly newsletters with weekly e-mail updates containing buy and sell recommendations. His information primarily featured details on buying call options. In addition to the one year $5,000 subscription price, I lost more money in the stock market that year than ever before or ever since.

People buy calls because they have read that buying them is the least risky way to invest and a sure way to limit your losses to the premiums paid when buying one or more call contracts. (One option contract is comprised of 100 shares of stock.) They hope the stock will go up, and they will make a profit, either by selling the calls at a higher price or by exercising their option (i.e., buy the shares at the strike price at a point when the market price is higher).

Buying one call option gives you the right (but not the obligation) to purchase one hundred shares of a company's stock at a certain price (called the strike price) from the date of purchase until the third Friday of a specific month (called the expiration date).

Let's look at a specific real world example.

Let's assume that you would like to own some shares of Dell Computer Company. As of today the price is 16.88. You are convinced that Dell is in a temporary slump and will soon resume growing. You'd love to own 500 shares. At 16.88 per share, 500 would cost you $8,444. That's more money than you have available right now. Maybe you could buy five call option contracts with limited risk. Checking the stock symbol for Dell computers, which happens to be DELL on the Yahoo Finance screen, or check it on any one of a number of financial research screens on your computer. You then find that you can buy five call option contracts (500 shares) with an expiration date of the third Friday in August. Since you strongly believe that the DELL stock price will increase over time, you decide to select the "strike price" for August call options at $17.00 per share. Even though that's twelve cents higher than the current market price, you believe the DELL share price will go much higher. You will notice on the Yahoo Finance DELL options screen that the premium you must pay for the right to buy DELL shares for $17.00 each is $1.27 per share. Your premium cost for 500 shares times $1.27 for a total of $635.00.

Example of a Call Option:

Suppose DELL's stock price is going to go up to $20.00 in the next few months. This would cost $635.00 today and when you bought the 500 shares of DELL stock in a few months at $17.00 per share your total cost would be 500 times your $17.00 strike price ($8500.00 plus your premium cost of $635.00 for a total cost of $9135.00). Now you sell your 500 DELL shares which currently have a market price of $20.00 per share for a total of 500 times $20.00 or $10,000, leaving you with a profit of $865.00 (broker transactions commissions not included). If the transaction doesn't work out and the shares of DELL instead drop to $15.00 a share, your option contract would have expired worthless in August and your maximum loss would have been the $635.00 premium you paid. Remember, buying call options does not <u>obligate</u> you to purchase the shares. It only gives you the <u>right</u> to purchase those shares at the strike price you selected.

I know there are many other ways you can deal with any options you have bought that offer the possibility of significantly higher gains in a short period of time. I have no experience with those various possibilities and will not pretend to know or write about them. There are many books available on various strategies and possible profits that might be gained as well as the risks.

Keep learning

Cellcom Israel Ltd. (CEL) is a provider of cellular communications services in Israel. Cellcom offers a range of cellular services through its cellular networks. These services include basic and advanced cellular telephone services, text and multimedia messaging services and advanced cellular content and data services. As of December 31, 2010, the Company also offers international roaming services in 179 countries. It offers its subscribers a selection of handsets from various global manufacturers, as well as extended warranty, and repair and replacement services. In addition, the company offers landline transmission and data services to business customers and telecommunications operators where it offers landline telephone services. As of December 31, 2010, the Company provided cellular communications services to approximately 3.394 million subscribers, including basic cellular telephone services and value-added services, as well as handset sales. In August 2011, the company acquired Netvision Ltd.

CEL is one of the most highly leveraged companies in the Communications Services industry and has a Debt to Total

Capital ratio of 97.05 percent. Additionally, the percentage of debt used in its capital structure grew this year. During the past year CEL's price per share has varied from approximately $32.00 to a current low of near $7.00. As of this writing the company's sales and income are declining. I own 1000 shares in CEL but do not have pending options on the stock. CEL currently pays a dividend of approximately 14 percent.

All of the above information and much more regarding CEL or any other company is available online free.

During the year long period I subscribed to the expert professional services, they provided me with specific recommendations for options I should buy for various companies. They were registered investment advisors and had done the research on those recommended companies. I accepted many of their "option buy" recommendations fully expecting that I would have a very profitable year with my investing activities. I paid thousands of dollars in premiums that year only to learn that most of the stock options I had purchased expired worthless on the designated expiration date resulting in me losing all the premium money I had paid for buying the call options. This taught me that I needed to learn more myself and not blindly follow the advice of so-called experts. Since I had lost several thousand dollars in premiums paid for the call options I began to wonder who received the money that I lost. (I also learned that statistically over 80 percent of all option transactions expire as worthless.) An unavoidable question entered my mind. When I pay the premium for buying call options, who gets that money?

I assumed it's the investor who employs the opposite strategy when selecting a company and selling options since that investor is paid a premium for every put contract sold. The premium money is immediately placed in the investment account. If on the pre-designated third Friday of the month your put option expires worthless you get to keep the premium you received when you sold the put options. (Yes, 80 percent of your put options will normally expire worthless. The other 20 percent will be assigned to you.) That means you are obligated to buy the shares at the strike price you determined and selected. That's why it is important that when you sell a put option on a stock, that you select it carefully on the basis of at what price you would like to own that stock.

In my case another criteria for selecting a stock for put selling is that it must pay quarterly dividends. I should caution you that before you begin a put selling strategy your online trading firm will most likely require that your account be margin enabled. This means in the event that an above average number of puts are assigned to you, at expiration time you will be able to borrow from your online broker in the event you have insufficient cash in your account to pay for the shares you obligated yourself to buy at the strike price. If, on expiration date, the cost of the shares you sold put options on is below the strike price, you will effectively be buying those shares at the strike price. Therefore, it's best to have sufficient cash in your trading account. If you need to borrow money from your broker you'll find that the interest the broker charges is not going to be to your liking.

The popularity of option trading has increased dramatically though it is not as well-known nor understood as simply buying and selling stocks. That said, it's easier than you think.

An example

The following is not a hypothetical example, it's an actual transaction I made in my own trading account. In searching for a stock I didn't already own (but would like to own) I searched for companies with stable earnings over a number of years and paying above average dividends. During this particular search I found Capstead Mortgage Corporation. (Stock symbol: CMO)

I learned that Capstead Mortgage Corporation (CMO), which was founded in 1985 with headquarters in Dallas, operates as a self-managed real estate investment trust (REIT). Capstead earns income from investing in a leveraged portfolio of residential mortgage pass-through securities consisting almost exclusively of adjustable-rate mortgage (ARM) securities issued and guaranteed by government-sponsored enterprises. As of December 31, 2011, most of the company's residential mortgage securities were classified as available-for-sale securities. The company qualifies as a real estate investment trust for federal income tax purposes. Since it operates as a REIT the company would not be subject to federal corporate income taxes if it distributes at least 90 percent of its taxable income to its stockholders.

I rarely buy a stock outright. I get the stock assigned by selling put options usually at a strike price slightly lower than the market price, plus I get paid a premium for selling puts which further reduces my acquisition cost. Over the past two years I have repeated this process with CMO three times and currently own 4,000 shares. Since a $1,200 dividend payment was credited in my trading account today, I wouldn't mind adding some more CMO shares sometime this year. Today's share price is $13.25 so I could buy an additional 1,000 shares outright at a cost of $13,250 plus a small broker commission. However, I use a different strategy. Instead I go to my Ameritrade option screen and click on "Research and Ideas"' followed by "Stocks." Almost immediately the research screen appears. In the upper right just below "Change Company" I type "CMO" and click "Go." Right away a screen appears with an incredible amount of research information on Capstead Mortgage Corp. The left portion of the screen provides a number of details. Since I already own 3,000 shares of CMO the only information I want to check is the current dividend the company pays. I see that the annual dividend yield is currently 12.83 percent. That's an attractive return if you are able to commit yourself to a possible purchase within the next few months. I've never bought CMO shares outright. Instead I used the option strategy of selling naked puts. Right now I'm going to sell six put contracts on CMO.

Back on my Ameritrade account screen I click "Trade" then just below that I click "Options." Immediately the "Options" screen appears. Directly under "Underlying Symbol" I type the stock symbol, which in this case is CMO. Next I click "Option Chain" to the right of where I just typed CMO. Immediately the CMO option chain screen appears.

I took my time to study puts. At first it looks complicated. (So did learning to fly an airplane.) Before long it begins to look simple. The Options Screen page is divided with Call Options on the left half and Put Options on the right half. The page is further divided by months. The first month listed today is May. In the upper left I see that the market price for CMO today is $13.72 per share. I scroll to the lower part of the page and click on "CMO Nov. 17." This means that the expiration date for any November option will be the third Friday in November, which is November 17. Then I only look on the right side of the page because I want to sell Put options. I know the price today is $13.72 and the price trend during the past several weeks has been on the rise for CMO. Why would I be looking at the November 15 CMO puts? If I place an order to sell ten put contracts on CMO, I'm obligating myself to purchase 1,000 shares (ten contracts) at $15.00 per share. That's $1.28 more per share than today's $13.72 price.

Okay, now we're getting to the interesting part. Why would I do that? Immediately to the right of "15.0 Put" you see $2.00. That means someone out there is willing to pay me $2.00 per share of CMO if I accept the responsibility of purchasing the CMO shares at $15.00 each. I mentally calculate that $15.00 minus $2.00 is $13.00. That's lower than the price is today. I would be happy to pay the $15,000 for 1,000 shares in November because when I sell the ten put sell contracts today I immediately receive $2,000 in my account (minus a small commission fee). Of course I make absolutely sure that I will have at least $15,000 in cash available in my trading account on the third Friday of November. I actually hope that, come the third Friday in November, the option will be "Assigned" to me. This means I will own 1,000 additional shares of CMO at a price lower than if I would have bought them outright some months earlier. That's because I was paid a $2,000 premium when I sold the put options. Of course if the price for CMO shares are higher on the third Friday of November my option "expires worthless" and I don't get to buy the stock but I do get to keep the $2,000 premium.

Since I want to add to my high-dividend-paying portfolio holdings, I repeat the whole process and collect some additional premium money. Okay, back to the CMO "Option Chain" screen. I click on 15.0 Put. Immediately a small screen opens showing: CMO November 17, 2012 15.0 Put. Just below the top line I see the "Buy, Sell, Set, Trade Trigger-Add to Watch List." I click "Sell." Next a new screen appears with "Options" on the top. Just below "Underlying Symbol" I see the company symbol CMO. The line below reads: "Action. # of Contracts. Option Contract." Under "# of Contracts" I enter the number ten since it is the number of CMO contracts on which I wish to place an order to sell in the November put options. Under "Option Contract" the CMO November 15 put is already shown. Below it is listed the following: "Order Type." I nearly always click on the small "down arrow" and indicate "Market." It means that my order will be executed immediately at the market bid price of the premium. If I don't select "Market" I will be able to fill in a price that is maybe a little higher than the bid price as shown on the "Option" screen. That makes it a "Limit" order which may or may not be accepted and filled. I click on "Market" and immediately, in green color, I see the words: "Review Order" which I click on. I now have three options: "Place Order, Change Order or Do Not Place Order." When I click "Place Order" it immediately shows the amount of premium money deposited in my account excluding the broker commission. To get the precise amount deposited in my account I return to the top of the screen and click "Accounts." Just under "Trading Tools" I click "History & Statements." I scroll to the bottom of that screen and see the details of my latest transaction including the exact amount of premium money, including the cost of commission, deposited in my account.

Research before investing

No prudent person would invest their hard-earned money without serious research. When purchasing a business or income-producing property that "research" is generally referred to as "due diligence." I'm not an investment advisor and will not pretend to be. I will only share with you what I attempt to learn about a company before committing to acquiring some of its shares.

1. I want to get an idea of the total debt load the company is obligated to repay over time. That's why I pay attention to the debt-to-equity ratio which is total debt divided by total equity. If, for example, a company has total debt equal of $15,000,000 and total stockholder equity of $10,000,000 it means that for every dollar of the company is owned by the shareholders, the company

owes $1.50 to creditors. This is listed as debt-to-equity ratio 1.5 times or 150 percent. A Debt-to-Equity ratio of 150 percent is nearly always too high to suit me and may indicate that the company is too deep in debt. Actually its liabilities are higher than the value of its assets. Normally, for individuals, when that is the reality we know that he or she is heading for bankruptcy. It's generally no different for companies (or for countries and governments). Whenever an entity spends more than it takes in it's heading for financial disaster unless cash flow can be increased significantly. Generally I shy away from companies which have price/earning ratios in excess of 1.5. If the company pays a good dividend and has adequate cash flow to service its debt load I might consider it after doing further research. When the company is operated as a REIT (Real Estate Investment Trust) a high debt owed by the company is, in most cases, acceptable because the actual value of their holdings is often not accurately reflected in their financial statements. In addition, companies operating as a REIT are required to pay at least 90 percent of their profits to their shareholders. Capstead Mortgage (CMO) is operated as a REIT with a P/E ratio of 8.14.

2. Definition of Earnings Per Share (EPS): Represents the portion of a company's profit allocated to each outstanding share of common stock. EPS serve as an indicator of a company's profitability. Calculate EPS by taking the net earnings and divide by the outstanding shares.

3. Definition of Price to Earnings ratio (P/E): Calculate the P/E by taking the share price and dividing it by the company's EPS. P/E = Stock Price ÷ EPS. For example, a company with a share price of $40 and an EPS of 8 would have a P/E of 5 ($40 ÷ 8 = 5). What does P/E tell you? The P/E gives you an idea of what the market is willing to pay for the company's earnings. The higher the P/E the more the market is willing to pay. Some investors read a high P/E as an overpriced stock which may be the case, however it can also indicate the market has high hopes for this stock's future and has bid up the price. Therefore I find it meaningful to look at other factors and continue my research.
4. I sign in to my Ameritrade account screen and click on Research & Ideas and then select "Stocks." This opens the research screen. In the upper right area of the screen, just below "Change Company Symbol" lookup I enter the company symbol CMO. The first screen I see is the corporate "Overview" screen. Watching the right side of the screen and scrolling down slowly, I see the recommendations of various research firms. The left side of the screen shows a number of important details including the company's Annual Dividend Yield, Price/Earnings ratio (P/E) and various additional details about the company stock. Next I select "Fundamentals" which provides me with the following information:

"Capstead Mortgage Corporation (Capstead) operates as a self-managed real estate investment trust (REIT). Capstead earns income from investing in a leveraged portfolio of residential mortgage pass-through securities consisting almost exclusively of adjustable-rate mortgage (ARM) securities issued and guaranteed by government-sponsored enterprises, either Federal National Mortgage Association (Fannie Mae) or Federal Home Loan Mortgage Corporation (Freddie Mac) (together, the government-sponsored enterprises (GSEs)), or by an agency of the federal government, Government National Mortgage Association (Ginnie Mae). As of December 31, 2011, most of the Company's residential mortgage securities were classified as available-for-sale securities."

Next I click on "Earnings" which yields the following details: *"CMO reported 1st quarter 2012 earnings of $0.44, beating the consensus estimate of the 11 analysts covering the company by 7.32%. The guidance had not changed during the year leading up to the announcement.*

For the coming quarter, analysts estimate CMO will earn $0.43 per share, a 8.33% decrease over the prior year 2nd quarter results".

Next I select "Financial Strength" and read *"CMO is among the most highly leveraged companies in the Real Estate Operations industry with its debt-to total capital ratio of 89.69 percent."* I would generally regard this high debt-to-capital ratio as undesirable. As a result I decide to investigate other stock research sites and I find that both the MS Money and Yahoo Finance research sites show CMO having a rather low P/E of 8.18. Since I understand a little about the balance sheets of

Real Estate Investment Trusts, I view the "financials strength" details differently when I invest in REITs as compared to other equities. This is especially a factor if the REIT I'm considering is a company owning real apartment complexes, shopping centers or other real estate. CMO does not own real estate outright. It is in the real estate financing business.

I usually check the "valuation" of a company as part of the research. That information pertaining to CMO provides the following information*: "Because CMO is in the Real Estate Operations industry and has positive earnings, the PE and Price to Book ratios are the most appropriate valuation measures. The Price to Sales ratio is less instructive than the PE since the company has positive earnings. Therefore CMO seems inexpensive with a PE value of 8.69, below the Real Estate Operations industry median PE of 12.68."*

As I'm writing this it's the third Friday of the month. That is always the day that any options trades I've placed during the past month or more. The third Friday of this month indicates that my options either expire worthless or will be assigned—meaning I will be obligated to purchase and pay for the optioned shares.

Approximately five months ago I decided to add some more shares of the big dividend paying company and sold 5 CMO Put contracts (500 shares) at a $12.50 strike price with expiration today. I received a premium of $688.17. The market price of CMO today is $13.35 which means I will not be assigned the shares. In other words I will not be purchasing the 500 additional shares of CMO today but get to keep the

$688.17 premium paid me at the time I placed the Put Sell order. This company is currently paying a near 10 percent dividend and is still attractive. Next week I will place another Put Sell order and earn another premium. I love the strategy and it has been exceptionally successful for me. Starting my online investment activities well past the normal retirement age, I feel very blessed that I have been able to learn and, over a period of less than fifteen years, grow my portfolio to a value in excess of three million dollars. I'm not boasting. I'm simply telling the verifiable truth.

I want to remind you again that I am not an investment advisor. I am simply sharing with the reader what I did to become successful and how I did it. I have found the following factors to be very important:

1. Only sell put options on stocks you want to own.
2. Don't let any temptation interfere with your pre-determined diversification policy.
3. If you have $100,000 available for trading, allocate approximately $10,000 to each transaction. In other words should all your put options be assigned, you will own the shares of ten different companies all of which you wanted to own.
4. By checking the market price of the company shares a week or two prior to expiration Friday, you will know ahead of expiration time your potential total cash requirement if some of your options should be assigned. No excuse for surprise endings.

Another strategy

My sister Mary, who is much younger than I am, occasionally would tell me about her IRA investments which were being managed by a local agent of a brokerage firm. Problem was, that instead of growing, the value of her IRA was gradually declining. When she complained to the agent he would recommend the sale of one or more of her holdings and replace it with others. Of course each time the agent made a transaction he earned a sizable commission. Frustrated, she asked me to look at the holdings in her IRA account. This was approximately ten years ago. Her IRA at that time had a market value of about $125,000. She asked for my advice. I recommended she open an online account with Scottrade which had a local office. Then she asked me to manage her IRA account for her. I agreed and promptly sold most of the holdings in her account. I wanted her account to be reasonably diversified and decided to invest approximately $6,000 in a variety of carefully researched stocks. Market value of $125,000 divided by $6,000 meant that her available funds would make it possible to select about 20 different equities. Since selling put options is a strategy not permitted for IRA accounts, I would select stocks based on two objectives:

1. Promising growing companies.
2. Companies paying good dividends.

In spite of losses during the 2008 market crash her account grew to a current market value of about $180,000. Mary will soon reach the age when she has to take a certain amount annually out of her IRA account. In the meantime she is supplementing her Social Security income by withdrawing $500 monthly from her Scottrade account. This monthly withdrawal does not affect the market value of her holdings because those holdings pay her approximately $6,000 in annual dividends.

During my business career I never invested in nor paid attention to the stock market. While I was still active in my various business entities I did increasingly turn responsibilities over to partners and team members. I was approaching the age of seventy when I tepidly put my toes in the turbulent waters of the stock market. Since I had a lifetime of experience in business I thought I'd quickly turn that experience to success. I was wrong and soon discovered that I had a lot to learn. Several investment-related books were purchased and studied, several meetings, seminars and "money shows" were attended. I subscribed to a number of investment advice letters written by experts. During the first few years I purchased shares of companies recommended by the various authors of investment letters. One well-known investment guru offered a subscription that would tell the subscribers which options to buy and when to get out of the transaction. As I stated earlier, the one year subscription fee was $5,000 and in spite of following this expert's recommendations, I experienced big losses during that year.

It was an expensive learning curve that convinced me that being successful in stock trading was not easy. I realized that I was one of the more than 90 percent of investors who buy stock in a company for a variety of reasons. Maybe I liked the products they manufacture or the opinion of an analyst who told me about the company. Stocks and the stock market are unpredictable and consistently picking winning stocks is impossible. Therefore I needed a strategy. If you want to be successful in the stock market (or nearly all other business endeavors) you need a strategy. Given my age I decided that I would build a portfolio by acquiring shares in highly rated companies that regularly paid above average dividends.

My goal was to build a portfolio that, over time, would deliver a steady stream of dividend payments, or "paychecks" on top of better-than-average capital gains. These days I won't even look at a stock or a fund unless it pays a steady dividend. Then, each time a dividend payment is deposited into my account I use the payout to buy additional shares—thereby compounding my original investment. Fortunately, you don't need to be an Einstein to understand why compounding has also been called an investor's best friend, or to see how you can profit from it. If you invest $10,000 in a security with a 7 percent yield, you will make $700 a year in income. If you take those dividends and reinvest them in the same security, your holdings would generate $982 a year after five years. After twenty years, your investment would generate $2,709 in dividends or 287 percent more than if you had not reinvested your dividends. Even if that security never gained a penny, after twenty years of reinvesting the dividends, your $10,000 investment in that security will grow to $38,697.

You are probably asking, "Where and how do I find a security, stock or company that pays a 7 percent yield? Below you will find the symbols of a few companies which I have in my portfolio as of this writing. Most I've owned for a few years. All are above average dividend paying stocks and represent only a few of my holdings. Please remember that providing you with this information is neither an endorsement nor a recommendation for you to purchase any of the companies. You need to do your own research and make your own decisions. Please note:

The dividends indicated were applicable at the time of this writing and may not be the same at the time you are reading this.

ETP	8.52%	ARLP	7.40%
FTF	7.20%	BP	6.30%
FTR	11.40%	CIM	16%
JHS	6.70%	CTL	8.50%
LGCY	9.30%	DX	12.23%
LINE	8.30%	EEP	7.57%
NLY	13.50%	EVV	7.79%
OHI	8.10%	EPD	5.43%
PGH	12.00%	ERF	15.94%
PSE	8.30%	AGNC	15.50%

Let me give you just one non-hypothetical example of how I acquired most of my holdings. I own 1,000 shares of stock in American Capital Agency Corp (AGNC). The company currently pays a 15.4 percent dividend. The price per share today is $32.30. I rarely buy shares of any company at the market price. When I did my research on AGNC I decided I wanted to own its shares because it was a high dividend paying company. Recently I did some more research on the company and, as I'm writing,

I wouldn't mind owning some more AGNC shares. To do this I went to my Ameritrade online account and clicked on "Trade" and then, just below Trade, selected "Options." Immediately the Options screen was displayed. In the square just below "Underlying Symbol" I typed "AGNC" and clicked on "Option Chain" which displayed the current month details. I ignored the left "Calls" side of the screen and concentrated only on the right side of the screen showing the information under "Puts."

My objective was to place a "Naked Put Sell Order" at a strike price somewhat below the current market price and, at the same time, paying me a reasonably good premium. In order to achieve that, I was willing to go out a few months in return for a larger premium. In this case the current month was June and I selected the September expiration price data. Remember, the option expiration date always occurs on the third Friday of every month. Also, please remember that this is not merely a speculative trade. I already own 1000 shares in this profitable high dividend paying REIT company (Real Estate Investment Trust). My mission this day was to simply acquire more of the stock at the lowest possible price. Looking at the September strike price and premium data, I look at the "32.0 Put." Just to the right I noticed that someone was willing to pay me $2.35 per share for my commitment to purchase the AGNC shares for a total of $32.00 per share on the third Friday in September. The $32 price I select is 38 cents per share less than current market value. Since my self-imposed diversification and cash management policy requires that my average transaction be around $12,000, I can place a put sell order on four AGNC

September $32 contracts. Each contract represents 100 shares. Thus I was obligating myself to purchase 400 shares of AGNC on the third Friday of September provided the market value of AGNC at that time is less than $32 per share. Then I click on the blue colored "32 Put." Almost immediately a small square overlay window appears where, in blue color, I see "Buy, Sell and two other choices which are not applicable for this transaction. I do NOT click Buy but instead choose Sell. This opens a new Options screen. Under the Underlying Symbol, AGNC is already showing. Under "Action" it shows "Sell to Open." Under the "# of Contracts" I type "4." Under "Option Contract" it shows, in blue color, AGNC September 22, 2012 32.0 Put" That means the expiration date of the contract is September 22, 2012. Under "Order Type" I click the small arrow to change "Limit" to "Market." Now scrolling down just a little I see, on a green background the words "Review Order." I click on that and see "Place Order," "Change Order" and "Do Not Place Order." This provides me with the estimated total premium that I will earn which is $956 (less broker commission). Now I have to wait until September 22. There are two possible outcomes:

1. The price of AGNC on September 22 is lower than $32.
2. The price of AGNC on September 22 is higher than $32.

Let's look at scenario ""1" where the price is lower than $32. It means that the shares will be assigned to me since I obligated myself to purchase the shares at $32. Even if the whole company crashed and burned and has no value at all, I would still have to pay the $32 per share. That is an extremely unlikely scenario but that's the risk. My cost will be 400 shares times $32. It is $12,800 less the $956 premium I received for selling four September 32 put contracts. Thus my cost is now $29.66 per share. Had I bought 400 shares outright today, at the market price, the AGNC shares would have cost me $32.38 per share. I would be very happy with scenario "1".

Now let's look at scenario "2". The price of AGNC is higher than $32. Whenever my put sell order turns out to be higher than the strike price, on expiration day the order would be "Expires Worthless." That means it simply goes away. I can't buy it. I don't pay a commission but I get to keep the $956 premium I received in my account when I sold the four put option contracts. Scenario 2 makes me happy as well because I will soon place another order to sell four AGNC put contracts for some future month's expiration date and I earn an additional premium deposited in my trading account. Since I want to add more shares of that company to my portfolio, I'll keep doing that until some third Friday in some month they will get assigned to me. Then I'll be obligated to buy the 400 shares and do so gladly.

In conclusion

I have found selling "Naked Puts" (selling put options on stock you do not own) is a great trading strategy providing you have enough money to pay for the shares of stock in case your put options are assigned or at least have sufficient cash in your trading account to cover the margin requirements.

The stock market is often turbulent and always unpredictable. I feel bad for those investors who have put a lot of their hard earned money into building an aggressive equity portfolio. I know they lose sleep on nights after the market plummets. Actually I look forward to checking up on my portfolio on bad market days. I also love to see dividends placed into my account many times a month and sometimes daily. Since I don't need the cash for monthly living costs, it increases my cash reserves and allows me to build my portfolio. I have friends who stress over their aggressive portfolios during the summer when markets can be more volatile. I understand because I've been there. There are numerous strategies for investing. Some fail, others succeed. None are risk free. Nothing in life is. I've outlined my strategy, which I've developed over the last nearly ten years. It's been very successful for me and more than tripled the market value of my portfolio. Best of all I never lose sleep over the ups and downs of the stock market.

Disclaimer

I'm not an investment advisor and I'm not affiliated with any brokerage firm, professional adviser or service. I do not recommend any online brokerage firm or company stocks mentioned in this investment chapter. They are simply companies whose shares I have purchased in the past, where and how I purchased them and, at the time of this writing, they are still in my portfolio. Each investor must do her or his individual research. Many readers would probably like to ask me questions or request advice. I'm neither qualified nor do I have the time to respond to any investment questions.

ABOUT THE AUTHOR

SID BARON was born in the Netherlands and immigrated with his family to the United States after the Second World War. He has enjoyed a successful career in starting a variety of businesses including a commercial FM broadcast station, electronic and telecommunication companies, a construction and development company and several others. Sid is still involved in many of the businesses he founded. In addition he has held leadership positions in various civic, church and charitable organizations. Currently he enjoys spending time with Margaret, his wife of sixty-two years, along with the families of their six children.

In 1970 Sid was diagnosed with multiple sclerosis. Through God's grace and his own proactive approach to managing the disease, he has been able to maintain an active lifestyle, which is something for which he is profoundly thankful.

From Humble Beginnings

Sid grew up on a small farm in the northern province of Holland. As a boy he experienced, first hand, what it was like living in Nazi occupied territory during World War ll.

After immigrating to the United States, and with very limited assets other than his own ingenuity, he started a number of businesses in various fields. Some of them expanded beyond his hometown of Bellingham, Washington to other states across the country.

The importance of all that success pales in comparison to the importance of family. Margaret and Sid have been blessed with six children, fourteen grandchildren and twenty-six great grandchildren. He has been blessed more richly then he would have dared to hope or pray for.

Faith, family and relationships are the values that count in life—far more than the accumulation of material possessions. He regards what he has achieved for himself as far less important than the opportunities he had helping others.

Anyone reading any of Sid's six other books will notice many continuing themes: Growing up in Nazi-occupied Holland during World War II, a depth of humor that keeps him from taking life too seriously, an abundant faith, dedication to family and friends, and living and thriving in life and business in spite of his over forty years living with multiple sclerosis.

Please visit exxelpublishing.com to find out more about Sid's books; or to make personal contact, email Sid at info@exxelpublishing.com